IF YOU WOULD NOT HAVE A MAN FLINCH WHEN THE CRISIS COMES...

...TRAIN HIM BEFORE IT COMES.

SENECA

KILLING COMFORT

THE OVERLOOKED PREREQUISITE TO EXTRAORDINARY RESULTS

JERRED MOON

First published in the United States by End of Three Publishing.

www.killingcomfort.com

Designed by Jerred Moon

Names: Moon, Jerred, author.
Title: Killing Comfort: The Overlooked Prerequisite To Extraordinary Results / Jerred Moon
Description: First Edition | End of Three Publishing, 2020.

Identifiers: ISBN 978-1-7348580-1-3 (hardcover) | ISBN 978-1-7348580-2-0 (paperback) | ISBN 978-1-7348580-3-7 (ebook)

Our books may be purchased in bulk for promotional, educational or business use. Please contact your local bookseller or the End of Three Corporate and Premium Sales Department at +1 214 513 3909 or by email at Support@EndofThreeFitness.com

First Edition: May 2020

DEDICATION

To William, Graham, and Eleanor may
you guard yourselves against indolence.
Do not fear a strenuous life; instead, pursue it.

CONTENTS

Introduction: To Begin   1

PRESS FORWARD AGAINST YOUR OWN DESIRE

     Chapter 1: 86% Failure   9

     Chapter 2: The Discomfort Effect   19

     Chapter 3: Daily Over Decades   24

Part 1: The Traps   28

THE TRUE COST OF COMFORT

     Chapter 4: Comfort   34

     Chapter 5: Prosperity   42

     Chapter 6: Ideas   54

     Chapter 7: Performance   63

     Chapter 8: Mind   70

     Chapter 9: Leadership   84

Part 2: The Truth   92

AVIATE - NAVIGATE - COMMUNICATE

    Chapter 10: Aviate   98

    Chapter 11: Navigate   107

    Chapter 12: Communicate   119

Part 3: Results   126

THE 86% PROCESS

    Chapter 13: Balance   131

    Chapter 14: Focus   139

    Chapter 15: Grit   147

    Chapter 16: Essential Habits   167

    Chapter 17: Mistakes   177

    Chapter 18: Comfort is the Enemy   189

On the Research   193

About the Author   194

Acknowledgements   195

TO BEGIN:

*PRESS FORWARD
AGAINST YOUR
OWN DESIRE*

KILLING THE RIGHT COMFORT

"You have the aircraft! You have the Aircraft!"

Feeling like I had just absorbed a punch from Mike Tyson, I relinquished control of the jet.

Captain Murrell took control of the aircraft and radioed for an emergency landing and as soon as the plane landed I was swept off to the hospital.

Seventy-two hours later I had surgery, and within 18 months, my flying days were over. My service career began in one of the most selective programs in the entire U.S. Military, Euro-NATO Joint Jet Pilot Training (ENJJPT).

And the question I still ask myself to this day is, "How did I position myself to get into such a selective program like ENJJPT?"

I didn't graduate from Harvard, didn't have an engineering degree from some Ivy League school, nor was I ever an Eagle Scout. The day I showed up for ENJJPT, I was sitting among men with these very accomplishments. From day one, I felt like I had to

2

work twice as hard as everyone else to stay where I was.

Looking back now, I realize there was only one thing I was really good at: **Killing Comfort.**

If that meant studying for 12 hours straight, I could do it. If that meant waking up at 4 AM to train, I could do it. If that meant skipping out on a party with friends to focus on my goals, I could do it. And, I could do it for years on end.

Getting to this point was a goal I had dedicated every second of my life to for four solid years and before that had dreamt about for 20 years.

I was in kindergarten when people would ask the old, "What do you want to be when you grow up?" question and as far back as I can remember, my answer was always, "I am going to be a fighter pilot."

I'll never forget the day I was selected for Euro-NATO Joint Jet Pilot Training.

I was about to walk into a class after having just studied for the last several hours. There was a test that day. Right before I entered the room, the Colonel pulled me aside and said, "Hey, I wanted to let you know that you were selected for ENJJPT. It's a pretty selective program, so good job."

I instantly got a surge of adrenaline and my hands started to shake. I couldn't believe it. A goal I set 4 years prior, and worked my ass off for, had just been attained.

KILLING THE RIGHT COMFORT

When I was the new kid in the Reserve Officer Training Corps at Texas Tech University, I was sitting in an office waiting to in-process, when this guy walked in wearing a flight suit. Ever since that day, I had my sights set on being a pilot and getting selected for a pilot slot, but I had no idea how to go about it.

While I was sitting there, I heard a few people talking about how that guy had just been selected for Euro-NATO Joint Jet Pilot Training (ENJJPT), so I asked what that meant. One of the cadets chimed in, "You want to be a pilot, right?" I said, "Yeah." He said, "Well, about half of the pilot slots each year will go to the Air Force Academy. The other half will be competed for by almost every kid in ROTC in every college in the U.S.. ENJJPT nearly guarantees you will become a fighter pilot which makes it insanely competitive." I said, "Cool, that's what I'll do."

He smirked and said, "I don't think you get it." "Get what?" I said. He continued, "Let me put this in perspective for you. Every year about 1000 people attempt to become a Navy SEAL. Of those 1000 roughly 200 will succeed. In the Air Force, there are about 1000 pilot slots given out each year. Of those 1000 only about 50 are ENJJPT slots and not all 50 will end up succeeding." I sat there just staring at him. He went on, "Look, I am not saying the training process for becoming a pilot is as physically demanding as SEAL training, but the selection process is perhaps the most rigorous in existence."

I got it. This was going to be hard and it was exactly what I wanted. I had set my goal.

Getting there was the hard part. Every activity I did, or did not do, had to pass the litmus test of "Will this move me closer to, or further away, from my goal?" It would mean a lot of sacrifice, hard work, and dedication.

It was a heck of a lot of work to get to where I was...and it had all been taken away from me in an instant by something completely out of my control. Sustaining an injury while pulling G's in an aircraft is something no one could have ever predicted.

Today, many people ask me what it was like to have a dream like this one ripped away. Most want to know what happened afterwards—how did I respond?

What did I do? I moved on. Immediately.

Recall, here was one thing I was really good at: **Killing Comfort.**

I knew the comfortable thing to do would be to start drinking, feeling sorry for myself, and continually refer to my time as an Air Force Aviator as the 'good old days.' And while I will make many references to aviation throughout this book, I am not stuck in the past. My best days are the ones I am currently living. The event that transpired, that took away my dream, led me into a life I love. I wake up inspired and motivated every single day.

Instead of wallowing, I moved on. I broke strength and conditioning records in Special Operations and grew my businesses to a level only 4% of entrepreneurs will ever reach.

Fortunately for me, I learned something in the process I knew could never be taken away from me. I learned how to intentionally pursue discomfort.

We all know that working hard or getting out of our comfort zone is beneficial. But why do some work hard and still end up with marginal results?

If all it takes to truly succeed is consistency and hard work there would be a lot more millionaires and six-pack abs out there. While consistency and hard work are big pieces of the puzzle, they are not the only pieces. In football, a team can work extraordinarily hard and still gain zero yards. It takes the right play, or work, to move the team forward.

So, that's where this book comes in. The concept of doing hard things is not new. Almost every religious or philosophical text makes a warning of becoming too comfortable; in sanskrit, the word *bhoga* is used to define and warn of overindulgence, the Bible references slothfulness as a pitfall to man, Stoicisms urges discomfort to garner perspective.

But, knowing what hard things to pursue seems to be the real challenge, or what I call the intentional pursuit of discomfort. The intentional pursuit of discomfort is not the same thing as simply putting yourself in uncomfortable situations. It's putting yourself in the right uncomfortable situations for exponential growth.

It all starts with the simple idea of killing comfort.

At its best, comfort has eased you into mediocrity. At its worst, comfort is literally killing you. It's time we take the fight to comfort.

This book is about the art and science of driving forward against your own desire, or what I like to call, Killing Comfort.

The pages that follow tell the stories of men and women who were just like you. Men and women who struggled with all that life demands, but found a way to push forward, albeit uncomfortably. You will hear stories of John F. Kennedy and Theodore Roosevelt, Andrew Carnegie and John D. Rockefeller, military commanders and gold medalists. There will be ideas from Emmerson, Robert Scott Falcon, Henry Ford, Thomas Edison, Carl Von Clausewitz, Napoleon, Benjamin Franklin, Nietzsche and Marcus Aurelius.

We will also look to poetry and films, ancient texts, and a massive amount of scientific research. I'll weave in my own stories and experiences as well as data from tens of thousands of people who have utilized the services of my company, End of Three Fitness, over the last decade. We will look under every rock and around every corner to help us master the right forms of discomfort that yield forward progress.

To kill comfort, we'll need to cover three domains: first, the traps that unknowingly lead us to comfort, next, the areas we need to focus on for discomfort to bear fruit, and, lastly, how to pursue those areas with fervor.

KILLING THE RIGHT COMFORT

Ultimately, we seek out each area in a desire to see extraordinary results. Almost any action will lead to some result, but we are after extraordinary results.

You know that is what you are after and it's what you deserve. That's why you're reading this.

So, let's unlock what's been holding us back. Let's mark off the prerequisite that is overlooked by so many. Let's **KILL COMFORT**.

1. 86% FAILURE

"The average person puts about 25% of his energy and ability into his work. The world takes off its hat to those who put in more than 50% of their capacity, and stands on its head for those few and far between souls who devote 100%." Andrew Carnegie

On October 15, 1999, underlying themes of rebellion were sparked inside of a generation when Fight Club, based on the 1996 novel of the same name by Chuck Palahniuk, made its debut. The film, considered one of the greatest movies of all time, was also filled with countercultural ideas and insight.

In one of the most memorable scenes, Brad Pitt, playing Tyler Durden gives Edward Norton, The Narrator, a horrendous chemical burn by first kissing his hand to apply moisture, then dousing it with lye.

TYLER: It will hurt more than you've ever been burned and you will have a scar.

NARRATOR: Guided meditation worked for cancer, it could work for this.

9

1. 86% FAILURE

TYLER: Stay with the pain, don't block this out.

TYLER: Look at your hand. The first soap was made from the ashes of heroes. Like the first monkeys shot into space. Without pain, without sacrifice, we would have nothing!

NARRATOR: I tried not to think of the words "searing" or "flesh."

TYLER: Stop. This is your pain, this is your burning hand. It's right here!

NARRATOR: I'm going to my cave. I'm going to my cave, I'm going to find my power animal.

TYLER: No! Don't deal with it like those dead people do. Come on!

NARRATOR: I get the point!

TYLER: No, what you're feeling is premature enlightenment.

TYLER: This is the greatest moment of your life, man! And you're off somewhere missing it.

In a grave illustration, the writer of Fight Club elegantly portrayed one of the biggest problems facing us today. We run to corners, to dark rooms, and to our devices, so we never have to focus on the moment or deal with discomfort. We run from pain and avoid uncomfortable situations at all costs.

This was not my takeaway when I first saw the film and watched this scene. It wasn't until much later when I started to connect the purposeful pursuit of discomfort to success. A look to nature reinforced this connection.

The wolf. While often portrayed as near-mythical beasts, wolves are failures. For centuries, the wolf has inspired legends around the world in spite of the fact that the one thing a wolf does more than anything else, is fail.

If you look at the numbers, 86% of the time a wolf steps foot on a hunt, it will fail. So 6 out of 7 times it comes up short, gets nothing, and goes hungry.

Furthermore, one victory doesn't mean the hunt is over because there is still tomorrow, the day after tomorrow, and the day after that.

Wolves fail more than they succeed but, despite their rare 14% success rate, they have a momentous impact on the surrounding ecosystem.

TO REMOVE A FAILURE

Wolves are amazing beasts, but only when you are learning about them on TV from the comfort of your couch. In person and up close, a wolf can be pretty terrifying.

So terrifying that, believe it or not, the National Park Service at Yellowstone National Park allowed the shooting of wolves, and even the poisoning of wolves, until a policy change in 1960 made these acts illegal. Between 1914 and 1926, at least 136 wolves vanished from the park; by the 1940s, reports of wolf packs disappeared as well. By the mid-1900s, wolves hardly existed in the 48 states.

It turns out that, when you remove an apex predator from an ecosystem, even one that only succeeds 14% of the time, it's still a big deal.

Today, we know why this is a problem because now we are aware of one of the most exciting scientific findings of the past half-century: trophic cascades.

In a 2013 Ted Talk, an investigative journalist, George Monbiot, explained the impact wolves have and how a trophic cascade works;

> *"A trophic cascade is an ecological process which starts at the top of the food chain and tumbles all the way down to the bottom.*
>
> *And the classic example is what happened in the Yellowstone National Park in the United States when wolves were reintroduced in 1995. Now, we all know that wolves kill various species of animals, but perhaps we're slightly less aware that they give life to many others.*
>
> *Before the wolves turned up – they'd been absent for 70 years the numbers of deer [elk] (because there had been nothing to hunt them) had built up and built up in the Yellowstone Park and despite efforts by humans to control them they'd managed to reduce much of the vegetation there to almost nothing. They had just grazed it away.*

But as soon as the wolves arrived, even though they were few in number they started to have the most remarkable effects.

First, of course, they killed some of the deer [elk], but that wasn't the major thing. Much more significantly, they radically changed the behavior of the deer [elk]. The deer [elk] started avoiding certain parts of the park – the places where they could be trapped most easily – particularly the valleys and the gorges, and immediately those places started to regenerate. In some areas, the height of the trees quintupled in just six years. Bare valley sides quickly became forests of aspen and willow and cottonwood.

And as soon as that happened, the birds started moving in. The number of songbirds and migratory birds started to increase greatly.

The number of beavers started to increase because beavers like to eat the trees. And beavers, like wolves, are ecosystem engineers. They create niches for other species. And the dams they built in the rivers provided habitats for otters and muskrats and ducks and fish and reptiles and amphibians.

The wolves killed coyotes and as a result of that, the number of rabbits and mice began to rise which meant more hawks, more weasels, more foxes and more badgers. Ravens and bald eagles came down to feed on the carrion that the wolves had left.

Bears fed on it, too. And their population began to rise as well partly also because more berries were growing on the regenerating shrubs. And the bears reinforced the impact of the wolves by killing some of the calves of the deer [elk].

But here's where it gets really interesting. The wolves changed the behavior of the rivers. They began to meander less. There was less erosion. The channels narrowed. More pools formed. More riffle sections. All of which were great for wildlife habitats. The rivers changed in response to the wolves. And the reason was that the regenerating forests stabilized the banks so that they collapsed less often. So the rivers became more fixed in their course.

Similarly, by driving the deer [elk] out of some places, and the vegetation recovering on the valley side, there was less soil erosion because the vegetation stabilized that as well. So the wolves, small in number, transformed not just the ecosystem of the Yellowstone National Park – This massive area of land -- but also its physical geography."

After Monbiot's presentation gained wild popularity, scientists debated if the wolf could truly be given so much credit since nature is infinitely complex with a multitude of factors for every action described above.

Part of their disbelief stemmed not just from the lack of data but rather the vastness of the impact. Could the wolf really do all this?

1. 86% FAILURE

Emerging data on aspen trees and the elk population seem to be pulling in the wolf's favor.

Even one of the biggest antagonists to the idea, Colorado State University's Natural Resource Ecology Laboratory Professor Tom Hobbs, admits:

"There is no dispute among scientists that removing the wolf from Yellowstone had vast ecological impacts on the park, but there is a disagreement on what happens when you put it back."

This scientific debate only adds to the myth and legend of the wolf.

For our purposes, we know that when you add a true leader to an underperforming team, everything can change. And you are the leader who is going to lead change in your life.

I'll admit the scientists have a reason to be shocked—it's pretty phenomenal to believe that one animal population can have such a significant impact on its surroundings by merely being itself. It becomes even more mind-blowing considering that this apex predator brings about such dramatic changes despite the fact it is such a failure.

EMBRACING THE SUCK

If you think this is the kind of book where I am going to tell you to keep trying because one day you will hit it big, you grabbed the wrong book. And, furthermore, the facts don't agree with that sentiment.

15

1. 86% FAILURE

Yes, wolves keep trying, and they ultimately succeed, or else they would die. The success they achieve lasts only as long as their bellies are full. That is not the lesson we learn from the wolf, and it is not how life works.

How many times have you told yourself, "If I just got that job..." or "If I just had that car..." or "If I just had more freedom..." And, when you actually got that elusive thing, what happened next?

You were on top of the world for two seconds only to find yourself still part of the human condition and then onto something else. You were too focused on the success you desired and not content with the grind and continual failures it took to get there. You were not comfortable with the discomfort of achievement. You only wanted the prize.

So, then, what do we learn from the wolf?

There is no doubt that a wolf, by its very presence, has the power to change an entire ecosystem. Yes, it is going to fail 86% of the time, and yet it still has the ability to change the world. The only way to modify your world is to improve yourself, and to improve yourself is a daily practice of discomfort. It is this daily grind that leads to the occasional 14%.

But let's get real for a second, are you afraid to get better? If I were to come to hang out with you for a day, how much would I see you working on yourself? Are you going to tell me you don't have time? That you have excuses? Are you not focusing on yourself and instead pretending to be a martyr for your kids, family, friends, spouse, etc.?

You may be wondering what this looks like. It looks like you not investing a second of your time improving yourself. Not one second spent on pursuing the discomfort that will lead to success. This lack of focus often comes from the stories we tell ourselves. We skip workouts, stop reading books, and quit taking courses and say it's for the family. You tell yourself you are helping those around you. You tell yourself you are acting altruistically.

Let me make this very clear—the act of Killing Comfort and getting better is not a selfish one. The act of getting better is a trophic cascade for your life, and it can change everyone and everything around you.

Now don't go and *try* to make a change. Intentionally *trying* to change everyone and everything around you every single day is exhausting. Wolves don't try. They don't sit around worrying about the course of the river or the increasing elk population. Wolves do what they know how to do, and that is to be an apex predator.

When you Kill Comfort, you don't try to change your ecosystem. Your ecosystem changes around you, you shift rivers, and you change your geography.

The wolf is comfortable being uncomfortable. That's what we have to learn and embrace. Things don't get comfortable. You won't finally "make it." You will not "arrive." But, you can get comfortable with imperfection. Imperfect daily action will give you a direction by dint of victories preceded by a lot of failures.

1. 86% FAILURE

Your daily life is not over-the-top happiness because of what you have achieved. Everyday life is a process in which we have to learn, grow, fail, put in the work, try something new, and fail again.

I have no secret for striking it rich or becoming famous. There is no secret formula to get the body you've always wanted or to reach the goals you've set for yourself.

But, there is a process. A process that must be applied daily over decades for it to work. A method of intentionally seeking discomfort to improve every area of your life beyond what you could imagine. The process is uncomfortable and it is different for every person.

This process is what we call 86%, and it hurts like hell.

While you should always strive to make an effort towards your goals, 86% is not about dusting yourself off and trying again. That adage has been played out for too long. I know you are, like I am, tired of hearing about it.

86% isn't about trying again. It's not about changing the things or people around you.

The 86% process is about changing yourself and watching the world morph to you. It's about embracing the suck.

When you focus on the 86%, you'll be face to face with discomfort daily. And that's the point.

2. THE DISCOMFORT EFFECT

**"We do not want our children to become a generation of spectators. Rather we want each of them to be a participant in the vigorous life."** John F. Kennedy

In Chicago, Illinois, on April 10, 1899, Theodore Roosevelt gave a speech called "The Strenuous Life," where he contended that Americans should embrace strenuous effort and do hard things for the betterment of the nation. In the opening remarks, he states:

"I wish to preach, not the doctrine of ignoble ease, but the doctrine of the strenuous life, the life of toil and effort, of labor and strife."

He goes on to say, _"to preach that highest form of success which comes, not to the man who desires mere easy peace, but to the man who does not shrink from danger, from_

19

hardship, or from bitter toil, and who out of these wins the splendid ultimate triumph."

Roosevelt had many different health problems as he was growing up and had to embrace new levels of discomfort over and over to make progress in his life. He knew these principles were the key to his success, so he shared them to help shape the nation.

Fast forward 61 years, and John F. Kennedy is touting a similar message specifically aimed at the physical fitness of our nation in a piece published in Sports Illustrated on December 26, 1960, entitled *"The Soft American."* Kennedy could see that technology was improving the quality of life for most Americans, but he was concerned by a more significant effect.

"Of course, modern advances and increasing leisure can add greatly to the comfort and enjoyment of life. But they must not be confused with indolence, with, in the words of Theodore Roosevelt, "slothful-ease," with an increasing deterioration of our physical strength. For the strength of our youth and the fitness of our adults are among our most important assets, and this growing decline is a matter of urgent concern to thoughtful Americans."

Kennedy went even further in 1962, when he found an executive order from Theodore Roosevelt challenging all U.S. Marine officers to finish a ruck march of fifty miles in twenty hours. Kennedy reissued the challenge to Marine General David M. Shoup, but more interestingly, he issued it to the American public through extensive print, radio, television, and display advertising. A call to arms for the American people. An open challenge of discomfort.

2. THE DISCOMFORT EFFECT

Forty-eight years before Kennedy's *"Soft American"* plea, a more solemn request was made by Robert Scott Falcon.

Robert Scott Falcon is also known as 'Scott of the Antarctic,' a naval officer and explorer, who died attempting to be the first person to reach the South Pole.

Holed up in a tent for four days during a terrible storm, he writes his last letter home and makes this final request to his wife about his son, *"Above all, he must guard, and you must guard him against indolence. Make him a strenuous man. I had to force myself into being strenuous as you know—always had an inclination to be idle."*

A father's dying wish for his son had nothing to do specifically with education, making money, or being healthy. His only desire was that his son be a strenuous man, one who does hard things and does not fall into comfort. It was not that he did not desire great things for his son. Rather, he knew great things would always come to his offspring so long as they always took the strenuous route.

This is the secret Roosevelt, Kennedy, and Falcon all knew —discomfort yields progress. Discomfort is a teacher; a litmus test for activities we should be doing.

Self-imposed physical discomfort teaches us how to press on when our minds no longer want to, and in a controlled, safe, environment.

2. THE DISCOMFORT EFFECT

Mental discomfort expands our boundaries and pushes us to new levels of success, no matter the venture, relationship, business, fitness, etc.

CHASE DISCOMFORT, SEE SUCCESS

So when you think about success, think about the discomfort. Discomfort will become how you prioritize everything and organize your effort to achieve what will genuinely make you grow.

It's easy to say, "chase discomfort", and if that was all there was to it, I could end the book here. You could go after things that make you feel uncomfortable and see results. There is some truth to this, but in the real world it's a bit more complicated. The challenge is that you need to find discomfort in the right areas and in the right amounts. You will need to prioritize your discomfort daily, and that is what we will explore, in-depth, throughout this book.

Unfocused and occasional discomfort will result in some progress. However, the growth you see with this type of effort will result in a linear progression and what we are chasing are geometric results. You don't only need to do something that makes you uncomfortable today. You need to put a focus on your discomfort, compounded in the same areas over decades. You may have to start small, but one area of discomfort will build on the next area, and as this happens, you will see more and more success.

When you see a successful person in any domain, there is no doubt they have been pursuing discomfort for a very long time. They sucked once, they got uncomfortable, kept at it and then they started to suck a little bit less. Over time, they went

22

from sucking to decent. After they were decent, they became good. They then went from good to great, and finally to world-class.

The key is daily over decades. Pursuit builds success. Continuous daily pursuit is very uncomfortable.

3. DAILY OVER DECADES

"Singleness of purpose is one of the chief essentials for success in life, no matter what may be one's aim." John Rockefeller

Being uncomfortable for a moment will yield minimal results. However, discomfort on a long enough timeline will produce serious results. This concentrated effort on discomfort is everywhere. Look closely, and you'll always find it.

CONCENTRATION OF EFFORT, FOR RICHES

Andrew Carnegie, in a passage called, How to Win Fortune, he gives some wise advice about how to craft your action and attention.

Carnegie says, "One great failure of young men is lack of concentration."

He goes on to say, "Every thought should be concentrated upon the one business upon which a man has embarked. He should never scatter his shot."

He then suggests a change to a typical rule we've all heard, "The rule, 'Do not put all your eggs in one basket,' does not apply to a man's life work. Put all your eggs in one basket and then watch that basket, is the true doctrine—the most valuable rule of all."

Perhaps in the greatest rags-to-riches story known to man, Scottish-born, Andrew Carnegie, went from nothing to an American industrialist who amassed a fortune in the steel industry. He went from a messenger in a telegraph office, to selling his empire in 1901 for $480 million, making Andrew Carnegie one of the world's richest men.

Andrew Carnegie was a master of concentrated daily action over decades and preached this philosophy for years.

DENY DISTRACTIONS, FOR GOLD MEDALS

In a 2018 study, a collection of ten Olympic, Paralympic, and World Championship gold medalists were asked what they believed contributed to their competitive success.

Interestingly, their responses had very little to do with a type of training, a specific coach, or how early in life they started practicing. Mostly, they attributed their successes to mental strength and perspective.

Each could transition easily between an immediate, performance-focused mindset and a long-term dedication/vision, which ultimately led to their success.

To help future athletes looking to succeed at a high level, the researchers asked the gold medalists specific questions such as,"What advice would you give other athletes?"

A recurring theme among all champions was staying focused, embracing challenges, and being comfortable going at it alone.

Elite athletes know that everyone they compete against has every advantage they do. They all have great coaches, they all have superior training programs and nutrition protocols, and they all have an unparalleled level of focus and discipline. You don't compete against other humans for a gold medal who don't also have these traits. Elite athletes believe it is something between the ears that gives them a competitive advantage and not merely hard work.

DAILY DISCOMFORT, FOR A BETTER LIFE

Likewise, we all have the same building blocks. We all have 24 hours in a day to shape our future and build who we want to become. However, some succeed at a high level, and others coast into mediocrity, or worse.

Today, you can have anything you want whenever you want. New technological advances are inspiring and impressive, but are we leading it or are these advances leading us to a life of slothful ease.

In life, the path to success is not different from what Andrew Carnegie and these gold medalists have laid before us; concentrate your efforts and limit distraction, embrace the suck, and get comfortable handling challenges alone.

But where do you start? What areas of discomfort will produce results? Of all the things you could be doing, what should you be doing?

Kill Comfort.

Explaining this idea is easy—living it can be tough.

Comfort is like a baby lion. You take it on as an adorable little pet and, in the beginning, loving and nurturing it is no problem. However, as the lion starts to grow, you have to feed it more and more. Eventually, you realize this beast was never meant to be your pet. That cute face that lured you in now has sharp fangs and paws the size of your head. Eventually, the lion will destroy you because that's what lions do. Embracing comfort is an insidious process that can shorten your life and decrease your enjoyment of it.

Before we dive into how to kill comfort in your life and, in order to make the most meaningful impact, we have to clear the weeds on comfort. Once we clear up all the sneaky ways comfort is creeping into your life and slowing you down, then we can tackle what killing comfort looks like and set you on the path towards a better life.

PART 1: THE TRAPS

THE TRUE COST OF COMFORT

COMFORT COSTS

In the 1986 film, Labyrinth, sixteen-year-old Sarah (Jennifer Connelly) is given thirteen hours to solve a labyrinth and rescue her baby brother Toby (Toby Froud) when her wish for him to be taken away is granted by the Goblin King Jareth (David Bowie).

On her quest to save her brother, Sarah encounters the Junk Lady, played by Karen Prell. When they first bump into each other, the Junk Lady asks Sarah where she is going and she replies:

Sarah: I was searching for something.

The Junk Lady: Well, look here (gives Sarah her favorite Teddy bear).

Sarah: (Shocked) Lancelot? Thank you.

The Junk Lady: That's what you were looking for, wasn't it, my dear?

Sarah: Yes, I forgot.

Next, the Junk Lady escorts Sarah into a room amidst a land of junk. When Sarah enters the room, it is a replica of her room back home, and she jumps on the bed with excitement. Sarah then checks to see if her dad is home and opens her bedroom door only to find the Junk Lady barging her way back in.

The Junk Lady: Better to stay in here, dear! Yes, there is nothing you want out there!

The Junk Lady then proceeds to shower her with her things. The Junk Lady offers Sarah her favorite bunny rabbit, doll, panda slippers, lipstick, and more. She is loading Sarah up with her favorite possessions. Sarah, a bit stunned, takes it all in and sits down to manage all her things. She loves all of these things and begins to play with each one. Then, in a moment of clarity, Sarah asks:

Sarah: There was something I was looking for?

The Junk Lady: Don't talk nonsense. It's all here. Everything in the world you have ever cared about is all right here.

Sarah (Read a passage from the book)

The Junk Lady: What's the matter, my dear, don't you like your toys?

Sarah: (comes to her senses) It's all junk!

The Junk Lady: (picks up a music box) Well, what about this? This is not junk, eh?

Sarah: (smashes music box) Yes, it is!

After smashing her favorite music box, Sarah is then freed from the spell of the Junk Lady and is able to resume her quest.

Sarah's time to complete her quest is finite. The Junk Lady knows this and tries to fill her limited time with things that are fun, but ultimately unfulfilling, removing anything that would move her forward on her quest.

Our time is also finite, and we, sometimes without knowing, fill much of it with frivolous things and activities that make us feel comfortable.

Now, we don't have a Junk Lady trying to lead us astray from our mission, but...we have entrepreneurs.

In 2016, I had an eye-opening conversation with Joe DeSena, Founder of Spartan and the worldwide Spartan Race, in which millions have participated. In a discussion on comfort he said,

"Every day, there's an entrepreneur out there trying to figure out how to sell us something to make our lives easier. And so what that does is that changes normal. And normal gets softer and unhealthier and fatter every single year. And we are uncomfortable going away from normal."

Entrepreneurs exist who will answer the call Joe is talking about, and they do it every single day.

What is that call? The marketplace screams comfort. How can you make my life easier? How can you make this faster? How can you do the work for me at the lowest cost?

Entrepreneurs have been making promises for millenia to get things done faster for you, make things easier for you, and do it more cheaply than anyone else can.

There is no conspiracy theory, and it's not their fault. If entrepreneurs didn't have a market for making our lives more comfortable and more convenient, they would fail.

But they don't fail, they succeed overwhelmingly.

The challenge we face today is how to navigate all of this. Inherently riddled with lies and false ideas, the pursuit of comfort will destroy you. Some products, services, and ideas make us more efficient. Killing comfort does not mean doing everything the hard way. I am not suggesting that you pursue each task in the most laborious way possible or not leverage the technology that is available to us today. However, it can be difficult to know when the wool has been pulled over our eyes. Often we don't even know how comfortable we genuinely are nor are we aware of the price we are paying for that comfort. The traps we face today are many.

TRAPS THAT COST US A GREAT DEAL

1. Comfort
2. Prosperity
3. Ideas
4. Performance
5. Mind
6. Leadership

Above are six traps...all stealing slivers of your success. Some of you are fortunate enough to have avoided all of these traps. Others of you have fallen for at least one, and a remaining few will have been snared by all six.

Next, I'll unravel how these traps sneakily imprison us and how to avoid falling into them in the future. Pay attention just enough, and you'll have a fighting chance at making a real change in your life.

4. COMFORT

"The backbone of surprise is fusing speed with secrecy." Carl von Clausewitz

It was 2014 and I was sitting in a hotel room on a business trip, staring at the floor. I was there because someone said I had to be, and I was working a job I didn't like.

Just a few years before, my dream of being a fighter pilot in the U.S. Air Force had been ripped right out from underneath me, so I left the military and got a regular, average, everyday job in the civilian world.

The job provided me with the income I needed to support my family. I had started my company, End of Three Fitness, but it was very much a side-hustle, generating very little revenue. I wanted nothing more in this world than for my tiny fitness business to make just enough to pay the bills and support my family.

But, I had no idea how I could build a business with no savings and no clue what the next steps should be. I had a family to support and time was not a luxury I could afford.

Also, believe it or not, very few people believed in me. In the beginning, the small things stung a lot more than they do now. I remember showing one of

34

my closest friends the first product I created and wanted to sell. His response was, "You think people will give you money for this?" and left me with some solid, "I wouldn't do it, but good luck if you do," advice.

Likewise, very early on, I showed my website to a close family member and told them people were subscribing to my newsletter to get new articles, and their response was, "Why would anyone want to read your blog?" Damn. That one hurt even worse than the last.

But, I blame the naysayers for nothing; the real problem was that I didn't believe owning my own business was even a real possibility.

It wasn't until this business trip that I had some space to think. I had been working at my new job for a few months when I got to meet my new boss for the first time. He was 22 years old, had just graduated from college a few weeks earlier, and also happened to be blood-related to the owner of the company.

Recall, I had just left the military as an officer, in charge of teams of up to 40 people, before that, I was flying multi-million dollar aircraft and to get there I had to study leadership for four years.

I tried so hard to tell myself to swallow my ego. Civilian life wasn't my world, and I needed to play the game. It was then when I realized three essential truths.

First, I wasn't a leader, not in this company, but of myself. I wasn't leading my family or myself in the direction I wanted to go.

Second, I needed to use my intelligence and stop pretending like entrepreneurship was rocket science. Up to this point, I had found that in entrepreneurship, hard work can still result in $0. Realistically, you take the wrong steps, learn the wrong things, and head in the wrong direction. I needed to work smarter.

Lastly, I realized I was comfortable and had no reason to become uncomfortable. I was sitting there waiting. I was waiting for someone to permit me to chase my dream. I was sitting there waiting on my big break. My family was taken care of, the job wasn't overly stressful, and I liked the owner of the company.

But, I was comfortable. I had no reason to rock the boat, and so I didn't.

INSIDIOUS COMFORT

Although most people believe comfort is ultimately a good thing, complacency is insidious. We have too many opportunities to settle, we get pacified, and we refuse to struggle against resistance.

Look, no one sits down and makes a plan for becoming obese. No one decides a dead-end job is perfect, and no one purposefully designs a relationship that leads to unhappiness.

These things happen. They creep in on us.

4. COMFORT

Every new rung you climb in the ladder of life is an opportunity to settle, to get comfortable; people stagnate in their careers and some athletes never make it to the next level. They, knowingly or unknowingly, get soft—comfortable. The second you embrace comfort is the second you stop progressing, even if you have made it pretty far.

Comfort is a sneaky thing. I could have lied to myself and continued for decades, as if I was noble for working a job I hated, to support my family. But I knew I wanted to do something different. A 2009 George Clooney film illustrates this perfectly. The movie is called, *Up in the Air,* and in it, George Clooney plays Ryan Bingham, a guy who travels around the country, firing people. In one particular scene, Ryan is firing a guy named Bob, played by J.K. Simmons, who has worked at the company for several decades. Ryan asks him this profound question: *"How much did they pay you to give up on your dreams?"* to which Bob responds, *"Twenty-seven thousand a year."* Ryan continues, *"At what point were you going to stop and go back to what made you happy?"* Bob replied, *"That's a good question."*

This scene hit me like a ton of bricks. Now, I'm not saying that you need to become an entrepreneur in order to be happy. This couldn't be farther from the truth. However, you should be content in whatever it is you *are* doing. If you aren't, your fire gets extinguished.

YOUR FIRE

We all have a fire in us. Whether you are aware of this fire or not, it doesn't change the fact that humans are born with an innate desire to improve.

The problem is, that over time, we suffocate this fire. The average American spends 3 to 4 hours on a phone each day. What *could* you do with this amount of time? Add that time up and you could have gone back to school, gotten a private pilot's license, started a business, and so much more.

You can look at your phone, binge-worthy video service, or any other time-suck as a giant pacifier shoved in your mouth— just like we give to babies who need to be soothed. Every time you pacify yourself, the fire you have inside is suffocating.

Who could you become? What could you do? What impact could you make? Most humans will go to their graves without having answered these questions.. You won't find out if you don't feed the fire.

We have the desire, but it's easy for us to get sedated.

THE GENESIS

Let's call it like it is, the unwillingness to pursue discomfort together with the hyper-comfortable lives we live, lead to laziness, sparking most of our problems today.

We refuse to produce force against resistance. An idea from the well-known book, The War of Art by Steven

Pressfield, is the best book written on resistance. To sum it up, here's an excerpt:

"The more resistance you experience, the more important your unmanifested art/project/enterprise is to you - and the more gratification you will feel when you finally do it."

On a basic level, if you feel you should do something, or desire to do something that matters, that is worth doing, resistance comes. We live in a soft world where you don't have to do anything you don't want to do. The existence of resistance cripples us.

This idea is no different than lifting a heavy load for increased strength. If you want to get stronger, you will need to lift a mass. This mass will resist your muscles through gravity. If you do it, you will be better for it.

The more you lift that resistance, for the long term, the easier it gets over months and years. You will have to move on to new challenges and meet further resistance if you want to continue to get stronger. Fighting resistance for progress rings true in the gym and in life.

Some people do not fight resistance at all, garnering little success in life. Others challenge resistance to a certain point and then get comfortable—never increasing the load. These are the people who achieve a moderate level of success, but who stop short.

The effort required to oppose resistance will be met with an equal amount of success. Never stop fighting resistance, never stop growing and never ever get comfortable.

THE BIRTH OF A PLAN

I killed comfort, quit my job, and started working on End of Three Fitness full time.

My first week as a full-time entrepreneur yielded $200, which meant my family and I were on the fast track to poverty. With nothing in savings, it made for some terrifying moments.

But, that fire I was talking about earlier, went from an ember to a raging inferno. I got extremely focused. I read a book a week, sometimes two. I would not allow for any outside distractions. I spent no time on anything other than business, fitness, or family. I was not comfortable, and it hurt like hell. I got extremely militant in my approach, which had friends telling me to chill out, slow down, and ease up. I didn't listen.

I killed comfort, which resulted in creating a business which is more successful than I could have ever imagined the first day I quit my corporate job.

To date, End of Three Fitness has helped over 15,000 athletes get better. Our products and services are making an impact that matters.

Now I look for where comfort may creep in, and I bat it away every chance I get.

Unfortunately, the cost of comfort is much greater than the cost of pursuing a career. And that is what we will cover next.

TAKEAWAYS

1. **Comfort is Sneaky.** Comfort is not merely sitting on the couch, watching TV. Look for areas in your life where you have become complacent.

2. **Feed your Fire.** Once you find out what your fire is, feed it! Don't let today's adult pacifiers extinguish your fire.

3. **Fight Resistance.** Finding your fire isn't the hard part. When you start feeding your fire, you will be met with obstacles and resistance— press on!

4. **Be Militant.** Don't let others tell you that your approach is too extreme—it may be the only way to get what you want.

5. PROSPERITY

"Caution and investigation are a necessary armor against error and imposition." Alexander Hamilton, The Federalist Papers

"Have a soft drink before your main meal."

"Sugar keeps your energy up and your appetite down."

"Sugar's quick energy can be the willpower you need to eat less."

These are all headlines from sugar ads from the late 1960s and early 1970s.

Have you ever heard something similar?

Maybe, _"It's just sugar; you'll burn it right off."_

Today we know that sugar is not a health food and that in excess, will cause weight gain and leave people saddled with diseases such as diabetes, obesity, and other chronic health problems.

But, I am not writing this book to educate you about sugar. I am writing this book to challenge your ideas and to make you aware of the hidden traps all around us. As we become more prosperous in society, things become more convenient, but at what cost? The trap of pursuit, more and more comfortable, is real.

In 2017, I interviewed Dr. Ben Bikman, a professor at Brigham Young University, about insulin resistance. He told me that insulin resistance is the single most prevalent disease worldwide. It masks itself, appearing in the form of chronic disease, specifically the chronic diseases, with the highest rates of mortality, that are most prevalent today. Dr. Bikman's research focus is on the mechanisms that cause and accompany metabolic disorders, such as obesity, type 2 diabetes, and dementia.

What struck me most was when he referred to the diseases he had been studying as the "Plagues of Prosperity." I had never heard it put so eloquently.

We have never been in a more prosperous and flourishing time in history, than we are right now. Yet, we are unhealthy, because most of the world is fat and sick.

According to the World Health Organization, 17.9 million people die from cardiovascular disease, which is an estimated 31% of all deaths worldwide. Smoking tobacco kills an additional 8 million people each year. I am not claiming that these two causes of death are entirely preventable, but simple lifestyle modifications can significantly reduce the incidence.

Now for a little context. In the 14th century, an outbreak of bubonic plague, known as the Black Death, claimed the lives of 50 million people over a period of 7 years. It was a catastrophic health event and that changed the course of history. Today, by comparison, cardiovascular disease and smoking kill about the same number of people every two years. The Black Death pandemic of the middle ages was eventually contained, but smoking and cardiovascular disease continue to wreak uncontrolled havoc worldwide.

Hitler committed genocide by killing an astounding 6 million Jews. We remember Adolf Hitler as one of the evilest men to have ever walked the planet, and his stance on human life was intolerable—so intolerable, that many nations waged war to stop this crime against humanity. Why then, when it comes to the number of deaths caused by heart disease and smoking, do we barely flinch?

Today, we can't point a finger at one man, or wage a war, but neither Sun Stuz nor Carl von Clausewitz could have theorized a more effective strategy for defeating an opponent than how we live our lives today. What is killing us today, in droves, is essentially a self-imposed genocide.

We like to eat, sit, and play on our phones and that's a problem.

Before I go any further, I have to let you know I am not a conspiracy theory guy. I don't think there is some secret organization out there controlling our steps or plotting our demise. I think what's happened is a result of an extreme technological advancement coupled with a human's innate desire to be comfortable.

But how did we get so blindsided by this obesity epidemic? How did we get so comfortable? In terms of metabolic disease, it will take generations to reverse the problems we are facing today.

EXPERIMENTS

So how did we get here?

The sad fact is humans are repeatedly used as test subjects in the marketplace and are generally unaware of this fact.

Don't think so?

Just take a look at cigarette and tobacco use. Tobacco use started as far back as 2,000 years ago, but it wasn't until 1795 when Dr. Samuel Thomas von Soemmering of Maine noted a correlation between lip cancer and pipe smoking.

During the 1920s, the first medical reports linking smoking to lung cancer began to appear, and a series of major medical reports in the 1950s and 1960s confirmed that tobacco use causes a range of serious diseases.

The tobacco industry used humans in a large-scale experiment and unintentionally proved that smoking is terrible for you.

Today, we are all part of a different widespread experiment, the one involving food.

In the late 1920s and early 1930s, right after those first medical reports linked smoking to lung cancer, refrigerators became commonplace.

5. PROSPERITY

New ways to store food kicked off an especially fertile time for creating new ways to process food. Much like any innovation, with the good comes the bad.

The phenomenal methods created to process and distribute food have helped millions of people around the globe. However, trouble started when the processing of food became more chemical and the processes involved became more and more robust.

So what's wrong with processed food?

For starters, processed food has fewer nutrients than its unprocessed counterpart. Furthermore, processed foods and beverages are the most significant sources of added sugar in our diets, an idea intertwined with Dr. Ben Bikman's research on insulin resistance.

But, I don't want to get into my opinion of processed foods. What does the science say?

In a 2019 two-week study, 20 adults presented with diets consisting of unprocessed or "ultra-processed" food matched for energy, macronutrients, sugar, fat, and fiber in a metabolic ward (perhaps the most rigorous research possible regarding nutrition) revealed some interesting data.

Those who ate the processed diet consumed roughly 500kcal more per day than those participants who adhered to the unprocessed diet, gaining both body mass and fat mass. Those participants who ate unprocessed food lost both body mass and fat mass.

So, why do we eat more food when it is processed, leading to the possible weight gain mentioned above?

The mechanism behind the weight gain is far more complex than simply consuming more calories. Hormones such as PYY, also known as peptide tyrosine-tyrosine, and ghrelin are responsible for our feelings of satiety and hunger, respectively. These hormones influence when and how much we eat. Participants, who ate the processed food diet ate these foods faster, had higher levels of PYY and lower levels of ghrelin, compared to baseline, than those participants who ate the unprocessed foods.

So processed foods are eaten faster and suppress appetite less compared to unprocessed foods.

Now, let's press pause for a second. I am not telling you the answer is low carb, paleo, keto, vegan, or vegetarianism. I am merely pointing out that food quality matters.

All the participants in the study who lost weight changed the quality of the food they ate. That's it! They took a step toward health by changing food type and not by adhering to strict diet rules.

So why would anyone decide to eat a processed food diet instead of an unprocessed food diet?

The answer is simple and also comes from the study. The study reported that the cost of the processed diet per kcal was 50% less than the unprocessed diet. Precisely because it's cheaper to get your energy from processed foods. Bummer.

Unfortunately, I feel that with food, we are where we were with the tobacco companies in the 1950s and 1960s. The research is becoming clear, but we have a long way to go. At least with smoking, when you tell someone to quit because it's beneficial for their health, they would save money!

With food, all we've got is that it's beneficial for your health to eat unprocessed food but it may be more expensive to do so. And, it's not a stretch to say that humans are willing to sacrifice their health for money. Most people would rather have the latest smartphone than spend cash on increasing their lifespan.

Spending more money on unprocessed food is an uncomfortable choice. If you think there is no way you can increase your grocery budget, you'll have to cut things out of your budget. Life may not be so cushy or comfy, but you'll be embracing discomfort.

Where are you on this spectrum?

On a more optimistic note, I will say that I think the good fight is being fought with respect to the quality of the food we eat. The more we decide to buy the healthy alternatives, the more the marketplace will adjust, and prices will come down. Anecdotally, I know when my wife and I first started eating healthier, around ten years ago, it was way more expensive than it is today. There weren't as many options, nor were there as many brands built to facilitate it. The needle is moving, however slowly, but it is moving. And you are in control every time you put food in your mouth. If you are willing, it's a simple, albeit not easy, problem to fix.

ON THE HORIZON

If cigarettes are on their way out, and the fight is being fought on the food front, what's next?

When it comes to health, I am always on the lookout for dumb things I am doing today that I think would seem absurd to the "future" me. What has me comfortable where I shouldn't be?

Flashback to 1920, when having a cigarette with a buddy wasn't considered to be dangerous in the least. The idea of smoke entering and exiting your lungs seemed innocuous. Now, we know it's nothing short of suicide. If I had been alive in 1920, would I have, even for a second, considered smoking to be a bad idea?

I think the next area of comfort that we need to deal with concerns our devices and their link to our mental health. It will have to suffice, though, to leave you with more of a thought experiment in this arena because the data is still emerging.

At a minimum, heavy usage of your phone or tablet leads to inactivity. If you add inactivity to the food problem above, the outlook is not good, but I am not going to drill that point in any further.

What I am more concerned about are the mental health challenges we are facing, and will face, as our dependency on our devices increases. New research says the average time spent on our phones climbed from 90 minutes per day to 3 hours per day just in the last decade.

So if you are less active due to a device, your chances for depression skyrocket.

According to Dr. Rhonda Patrick, several observational studies have found that physically active people are less likely to develop depression. For example, a Mendelian randomization study, a type of research method that provides evidence of links between modifiable risk factors and disease based on genetic variants within a population, demonstrated that higher levels of physical activity might be causally linked with a reduced risk for depression.

Also, numerous randomized-controlled trials have found that exercise mitigates depressive symptoms, facilitates recovery from depressive disorders, and prevents relapse.

For example, a meta-analysis of 25 randomized controlled trials comparing people who exercise to control groups found that exercise reduced depressive symptoms, and this effect was particularly strong for moderate- to vigorous-intensity aerobic exercise.

Research also found that teens who spend five or more hours per day on their devices are 71% more likely to have one risk factor for suicide. According to the CDC, suicide is one of the top 10 leading causes of death in the U.S. and is on the rise.

Yet, there is too much here to unpack and too many unknowns. As I said before, this is a thought experiment I have to leave you with. Do we blame social media? Is it something about the device itself? Is it simply inactivity?

Right now, we are at the "correlation is not causation" point. We can not definitively say that a rise in phone usage over the last decade causes mental health problems and an increase in the incidence of suicide. We can say they are correlated but not scientifically linked.

And that's fine. We can wait for another large-scale human experiment to run its course, and then we can start making definitive claims in 50 to 60 years.

In the meantime, I think I'll put my phone down more often, pick up a kettlebell, or write books, and spend time with my family. And, if I am wrong about the whole phone thing, I won't ever regret diverting my attention away from it and towards physical activity, intellectual pursuits, and spending time with my kids.

I am so thankful to be alive in a time of such prosperity and abundance. We can do anything, be anything, and have anything we want. It truly is a fantastic time to be alive. But each generation comes with its own set of problems and pitfalls, and none are immune. And, like every other time in history, there is no instruction manual on how to navigate your day-to-day life. Don't let the call of comfort and prosperity lead you into a large scale human experiment.

TAKEAWAYS

1. **Awareness.** Humans are self-destructive. Always be on the lookout for the latest idea that will be to your detriment.
2. **It's all connected.** There is no single lever to pull. Be mindful of how every action relates to another.
3. **You are in control.** Ownership is uncomfortable. Success, or failure, is on your shoulders.

I know this was a heavy chapter, so let me leave you with something a bit more lighthearted that could help guide you.

Famous comedian Jerry Seinfeld, often tells a joke about humans, dogs, and aliens. He puts it this way, "Dogs are the leaders of the planet. If you see two life forms, one of them's making a poop, the other one's carrying it for him, who would you assume is in charge?"

If an alien was to watch us eat processed foods proven to lead to a premature death, instead of unprocessed foods, what would they think? They might, mistakenly, think that we had no other choices! They would never conclude that we picked the processed food because we didn't want to make a hard choice like adjusting our budget.

Likewise, if an alien was to watch you, neck bent, and thumbs flying on your phone for hours each day, what assumption would they make? Who's in charge? Us or the device?

5. PROSPERITY

It's all simple. None of it is easy.

6. IDEAS

"*When science learns to understand human nature, it will be able to bring a happiness into our lives which machines and the physical sciences have failed to create.*" Bertrand Russell

In 1961, poet Donald Hall, published a book entitled *String Too Short To Be Saved* about his childhood summers spent in New Hampshire.

In one story, Hall recalls, "A man was cleaning the attic of an old house in New England, and he found a box which was full of tiny pieces of string. On the lid of the box, there was an inscription in an old hand: 'String too short to be saved.'"

In that simple illustration, Hall captured a metaphor for much of our lives. For what purpose would you hold onto a string that could serve no utility in your life? Likewise, we cling to stories and ideas that do not help us. Most of us have too many strings too short to save.

Although many believe skepticism is extremely valuable, always being a skeptic will come at a cost because some ideas are not worth holding onto. Skepticism is comfortable.

ONE OF MY STRINGS TOO SHORT TO BE SAVED

In 2010, I found one of my strings that was too short to save when I had the opportunity to work for a very wealthy entrepreneur, who later became my mentor.

My first day on the job, she sat me down and said, "The one thing I want you to get out of working here is learning."

She then walked me into a few rooms filled with books, sets of CDs, workbooks, and even cassette tapes.

I started looking around and was baffled. Every "scam" you had ever seen watching late-night TV infomercials and ads were in these rooms—she bought into them. Like all of them.

I saw a lot of "get rich" type training videos and books all around me. Stuff that I had always discounted. I even found myself starting to wonder if my mentor knew she had been duped.

But I quickly realized that it was I who had been duped. Up to this point, my extreme skepticism had me swindled.

My mentor used her best judgment when buying all these courses and she trusted the creators, not an easy thing to do. All she was trying to do was shortcut her learning curve to success by buying into information created by other successful people. She bought things I had thought were a scam for sure. But, her track record over a short, 10-year time period proved she was doing it right, and I was doing it wrong.

I decided then and there I was going to give being more like her a whirl, and I got my chance a few weeks later.

At that time, I was trying to grow my online business. I was bootstrapping everything and making very little money. I was betting I could Google and YouTube my way to success. Then, an offer came up to purchase an online digital marketing course for $2,000.

It was money I didn't have, and when I saw the ad and the sales page, my skepticism jumped right in.

You know the drill—all the typical skepticism stuff to try and protect my time and money. But, I remembered my recent life lesson, did my research on the course creator, and bought the course.

It was terrifying to spend that much money on information. But I did it. I took the entire course, did every step, watched every video and guess what, it worked!!

Within one month of finishing the course, I had made back my $2,000 investment. Within six months, I had 10×'d my $2,000 investment. That single course did way more for me than help me grow my business. It made me willing to invest in myself. It helped me drop my overall level of skepticism about a lot of things, and that's when my life started to take off.

CLEARING THE FOREST

Here are a few ideas for you...

The most significant wealth is wisdom.

The safest investment is an idea.

The best opportunity requires vision.

Success alone is impossible.

To make ideas like this stick, we have to clear away what is unnecessary. If a farmer wants to clear a field for planting, the first thing he does is cut down the trees and get rid of anything that isn't helpful for the development of the crop.

The "trees" in a journey to success are negative thoughts, self-doubt, and your old ideas "not worth saving." For anyone to achieve success, you have to become a lumberjack. You have to remove all the obstacles. We can talk about productivity, efficiency, and strategy all day but every attempt in these areas will be futile if you plant a seedling in the shade of an oak tree.

The oak will overshadow the seedling. Its deep roots will steal all the water and nutrients away. Any meager growth achieved will quickly be sapped by the oak left in the field. You cannot tolerate a negative mind *and* a lack of confidence. You have to uproot those oaks at the deepest level. It will not be easy, and it will take time, but it is 100% necessary. So, how does one do this?

6. IDEAS

Things to remember: 1. We are not our thoughts. Our thoughts come into our minds, and we believe that because they are in our minds, they are us. However, they are just thoughts. Thoughts lots of us have had. Thoughts are like air though. We breathe the air in, but it is not us. We use it how we need it then, we discard it. We can have negative thoughts and old ideas, but we do not have to accept them as factual. 2. Thoughts are habits. You have to train yourself how to think. You have to become disciplined in your mind. Control your thoughts each day.

So, how do we control our thoughts...

...the same way you create any new habit. You do not need to be perfect, and you do not need to control every thought—such an idea is not possible. You need to start small. Begin with just 5 minutes each day and purposely think thoughts you want to believe. Think of the life you want, how that will make you feel. Think of the person you are and who you are becoming, and how that makes you feel. The power of "thinking positively" is overrated. Still, I say practice controlling your thoughts for a small period of time by focusing on what you desire, and you will train yourself to become better.

Most thoughts are random or a reaction. Make them yours.

Own your thoughts. Control your mind.

You can chase after money, but it cannot be the end game. Make yourself indispensable and continually go the extra mile, and you will not fail.

DOGMATISM VS. SKEPTICISM

The opposite of skepticism is dogmatism, or the tendency to lay down principles as incontrovertibly true, without consideration of evidence or the opinions of others.

Being overly dogmatic or skeptical will stunt any potential growth.

Don't get me wrong. I am not saying to walk blindly into situations and refuse science or the analytical mind. Instead, I am asking you to be more aware of your ideas and their utility in your life.

A healthy level of skepticism keeps you from buying packages of cold air from the back of a guy's minivan during the summer.

An unhealthy level of skepticism leads to missed opportunities and a small life. If you pride yourself on your skepticism, you've probably missed out on a lot of great opportunities and protected yourself from very little.

Skepticism permits you to stay safe, to avoid trying new things, and is a way out of almost anything.

Stories and ideas have been handed down from generation to generation since time began. Some stories and ideas are retold because they are meant to protect us—to save us from pain and frustration.

These types of stories have served humanity for a long time by protecting us from danger by example rather than by advice.

6. IDEAS

Humans love a good story. Given our nature, it's almost impossible for us not to insert ourselves into any story and, consequently, our brains fully engage because the stakes are high! As a result, it's much easier for us to remember a story rather than a simple rule to follow.

This process has served humanity well for a long time. However, the dangers to life and limb in our day and age have dropped quite a bit. The fact of the matter is, because we don't face the same risks as our ancestors have in the past, we don't need their old stories.

We've all heard the story of the boy who cried wolf.

The tale concerns a shepherd boy who repeatedly tricks nearby villagers into thinking wolves are attacking his flock. When a wolf actually does appear, and the boy again calls for help. The villagers believe that it is another false alarm, and the wolf eats the sheep.

A story like this keeps our moral compass on track and protects us from the proverbial wolves. In spite of that, stories are still told to keep us from danger in our nerf world. New stories have emerged. Perhaps, in your family, there was an uncle who decided to invest all his money in the stock market. All was well until the stock market crashed and he lost all of his money. Or maybe you heard the story of a marathon runner who ran so hard he damaged his heart and died. Or perhaps you listened to some other story that is keeping you from taking action—maybe a story that is keeping you in the safe zone. These stories, even if they are true, are irrelevant. They are the exceptions, not the rule. Nevertheless, we hear these stories and they keep us from taking action. You can hear them on the news, from your parents, your friends, the internet...these stories are everywhere.

THE SKEPTICISM SWEET SPOT

So, where does this leave us?

On one hand, I am asking you to abandon skepticism and the old ideas that are hindering your progress. On the other hand, I am telling you not to be overly dogmatic and to still use your analytical brain.

It's effortless and comfortable to question the credibility of something and to be immediately dismissive of a new ideal, i.e., skepticism. It's also easy and comfortable to hold onto your current ideas without consideration of evidence or the opinions of others, i.e., dogmatism.

This leaves us with the pursuit of discomfort. Letting go of an idea is uncomfortable, doing the research to challenge your thoughts is painful and will leave you somewhere between dogmatism and skepticism.

TAKEAWAYS

1. **Identify your "strings too short to be saved."** What ideas or stories are you holding onto that are holding you back?

2. **Find the sweet spot.** Avoid dogmatism and skepticism. Hold onto ideas just tightly enough so as not to lose them, but not so tightly such that they can't be lost.

3. **Put in the work.** Finding answers and challenging ideas is uncomfortable and hard work. Do it anyway.

7. PERFORMANCE

"If you run with the lame, you will develop a limp" Louie Simmons

In the aviation world, there is a guideline known as the 60:1 rule.

The rule states that if you are just a single degree off your designated course, you will miss your target by 92 feet, for every mile you fly. This amounts to one full mile off course for every 60 miles you travel. So the greater distance you travel, even if just a single degree off course, the further you will be from your target.

So with that in mind, I'd like to ask you a question: how many degrees off course are you from being fully optimal?

Many people optimistically believe they are operating at a high level. However, they are entirely unaware that their current "A" game is more like their "C" game because of simple and often overlooked, everyday choices.

It turns out bringing your real "A" game is a daily discipline that develops over decades. In this chapter, my only goal is to open your mind to the fact that you may be off course, veering away from your true potential. Later in the book, we will discuss ways to get you back to optimal.

TO STOP A MOVING TRAIN

I live relatively close to train tracks and often have the unfortunate opportunity to watch a very long train, stop. It doesn't take a lesson in physics to understand that it takes a great deal of time to stop a train that weighs millions of pounds, safely.

While sitting in my car, I've watched a train braking, moving ever slower and slower until it is barely moving, then, just like that, it has stopped.

Our biological systems, i.e., our bodies, are not much different. Our body is a fascinating organism that is continually adapting to whatever we are doing. It takes a long time for our bodies to stop working properly.

Our body will make its best attempt, over and over, to adapt to a poor health decision. However, you are merely slowing yourself down one wrong choice at a time. You are slowing down, but the fact that you are still moving makes you think everything is still OK...until, that is, your pancreas says screw this, "I'm out!"

FAR FROM OPTIMAL

A 2007 study by Lamond et al., conducted at Centre for Sleep Research at University of South Australia investigated the processes of recovery over five days to normal cognitive function with respect to the number of sleep hours following 1 or 2 nights of total sleep deprivation

The results showed that just one night of a 9-hour sleep was enough for the subjects' response speed,

64

lapses, and feeling of sleepiness to return to the baseline, which is good news! This tells us, if you have only suffered 1 to 2 days of poor/no sleep, one 9-hour stretch can bring you back to normal.

However, if 9 hours of sleep is not a possibility for you, the outlook is a bit more grim.

The same study showed that after sleep deprivation and a 6-hour sleep night recovery, participants' performance, and feeling of sleepiness failed to return to the baseline. There wasn't a continual decline when sleeping only 6 hours each night, rather, there was a lower-than-initial but steady level of performance, i.e., a new normal.

Many other sleep studies have proven the human brain can, to some extent, adapt to a "new normal" following a period of poor sleep.

My aim here is not to preach the importance of sleep nor is it to dive deep into the science and mechanisms behind sleep. If you are seeking depth on this topic, I recommend any work by Dr. Matthew Walker. He is an expert in the intricacies of sleep and the overall benefits of sleep to your health, well-being, athletic recovery, happiness, and much more. Spoiler: Sleep is essential.

Now the previous study is a bit extreme because the participants were fully deprived of sleep for either one or two nights, so they did not get to sleep at all, which isn't usually the case for most of us.

So what about something a little more realistic?

7. PERFORMANCE

A 2019 study by Anna M. Beres, Jagiellonian University, found very similar results but used a longer timeline with less aggressive sleep deprivation.

In this study, participants' attention levels were assessed using a Stroop Color and Word Test. In a Stroop test, respondents must try to say the color of a word rather than read the word itself (or vice versa). For example, suppose the word *red* is written using green ink. Test takers then attempt to say "green" (the color) instead of *red* (the word). It can get difficult.

In this study, a "sleep deprivation" state for all participants was defined as about 5h21m of sleep. So not a night of no sleep, rather a few nights of decreased sleep.

During the recovery phase of the study, participants slept, on average, 7h33m each night for one full week. One of the most interesting findings concerns the recovery time necessary to get back to the reported baseline. Beres states, "The neurophysiological responses are heavily affected after a period of sleep deprivation, with one week of recovery being insufficient to return to a pre-testing performance of an individual."

To recap, going from 5 hours of sleep for several nights back to 7 hours for several more nights was not enough to bring the participants back to their original baseline.

Additional studies have tested both subjective and objective responses using something similar to the Stroop test. In these studies, participants subjectively think they are performing better and better in a sleep-deprived state yet, in reality, they are objectively performing worse and worse. There exists a vast amount of information on the effect sleep has on physical performance and its effect on mental performance.

But, instead of focusing on sleep and physical performance right now, let me make one quick mention of alcohol use and its effects on physical performance. Much like sleep, the studies and research on alcohol use are extensive.

I do, however, want to bring your attention to one study, conducted by Nemanja Lakićević from the Department of Psychological, Pedagogical and Educational Sciences, University of Palermo, Italy: The Effects of Alcohol Consumption on Recovery Following Resistance Exercise: A Systematic Review.

If you are unfamiliar with the term, a systematic review is essentially a study of studies. It's a summary of multiple studies which results in highly valid and specific conclusions. Systematic reviews sit at the top of the evidence-based hierarchy of information quality. In this particular review, over 20 different studies are included.

A significant takeaway deduced from this systematic review is that regular ingestion of alcohol is bad for recovery and performance. Alcohol has unfavorable effects on muscle protein synthesis, sleep quality, and several important hormones.

To get even more granular, the review takes a look at how long it takes for strength to get back to baseline after ingesting alcohol.

7. PERFORMANCE

Participants reporting the quickest recoveries stated that 24 to 48 hours was required to return to baseline, with some reporting 72 or more hours were necessary. One study reported it took an entire five days for strength to be returned to baseline.

Now, just for a minute, let the sleep and alcohol data settle in while also processing this "new normal" idea.

Good?

TO START A MOVING TRAIN

I don't bring up the topic of alcohol to convince alcoholics or people with a real drinking problem, to stop. That's a disorder that goes beyond the scope of this book. Neither am I urging insomniacs to get help.

However, I have worked with thousands of people, all around the globe, who are awesome humans. They are ambitious, they are fathers and mothers, and they enjoy fitness.

However, I see one or both of these habits prevalent in a majority of those I have worked with. They don't sleep enough and they drink what is considered a very small to moderate amount of alcohol.

And for these reasons, they are not functioning optimally. What's worse, they are unaware.

Sleeping 5 to 6 hours a night while also ingesting 1 to 2 alcoholic drinks, a few times a week, is fairly typical in today's world but keeps you at a mental and physical disadvantage. You aren't thinking as well as you could be, and you aren't as physically capable as you could be.

Now, I'd like to ask you the same question I asked at the beginning of the chapter: how many degrees off course are you from being fully optimal?

Are you on the slowing train but fooled because even some forward movement is still progress?

TAKEAWAYS

1. **Pursue optimal.** You may be unaware of how awesome you can be. Pursue optimal and find out.

2. **Sleep more.** Somewhere between 7 to 9 hours seems to do it for most people.

3. **Ditch the alcohol.** Its adverse effects far outweigh any of its benefits. Drinking alcohol for the antioxidants? I would hope you know there are at least 100 other ways to get antioxidants into your diet with absolutely no downside, i.e., eat vegetables.

The good news is that, while it takes time, everyone can make it back to baseline or better. You can go from a slowing train to one that's picking up speed or even going full steam ahead in the most optimal way.

8. MIND

"Whether you think you can, or you can't — You're right." Henry Ford

Thirteen years and nearly $3 billion.

That's how much time and money The Human Genome Project (HGP) took to complete.

The Human Genome Project sequenced and mapped all of the genes, together known as the genome of Homo sapiens. Now, we can read nature's complete genetic blueprint for building a human being.

This is no small feat.

Dr. Francis Collins, a physician-geneticist who discovered the genes associated with several diseases and led the Human Genome Project said,

"Decoding the human genome sequence is the most significant undertaking that we have mounted so far in an organized way in all of science. I believe that reading our blueprints, cataloging our instruction book, will be judged by history as more significant than even splitting the atom or going to the moon."

Other professionals have also said the mapping of the human genome is more monumental than the invention of the wheel.

And you are seeing the result of this today. At this very moment, you can send a saliva sample to a lab, pay a nominal fee, and gain insight into your own genetics.

With a simple test, you can find out if you have a predisposition to aerobic exercise or strength exercise, or even if you are at risk for certain diseases. It's impressive stuff.

But what if I told you that your brain doesn't care that much?

In 2018, 223 participants were recruited for a genotype study. They were signing up for a year-long "personalized health" study where they'd learn about the best exercises and diets for themselves, based on their genotype.

But, in reality, they were signing up to be lied to. Participants across the studies were told they had either the "good" version or the "bad" version of specific genes related to exercise performance, obesity risk, and other genes. So what was the lie?

Half of the people with "good" genes were told they had bad genes, and half of the people with "bad" genes were told they had good genes.

The study was pretty straightforward from here. They would feed participants a standardized meal to control for performance related to macronutrient intake and they took a baseline test. Then, a week later they took the test again after they were informed, or should I say misinformed, about their "good" or "bad" genes.

In both studies, beliefs about one's genes impacted both perceptual and physiological measures. In some cases, people who were told they had the bad version of a gene had worse outcomes in the second test than the first test. In other cases, people who were told they had a good version of a gene performed better in the second test than the first test, regardless of their actual genetics.

Having "bad" genes has been a long-standing excuse for decades. Plainly, a person thinks that, due to their specific set of genes, they cannot make progress.

Emerging evidence, in a somewhat new field of study called epigenetics, is proving that lifestyle and environmental factors can expose a person to pressures which prompt chemical responses. Things like a proper diet and exercise mediate positive epigenome change. The opposite is true of a poor diet and inactivity.

Epigenetics means, to a degree, that through diet and exercise, you can change how the genes you already have, get expressed.

Look at it this way, you are born with a specific set of genes, and you cannot change that fact. However, if you were given genes equivalent to an old, rusty, and broken down Honda Civic, that doesn't mean you can't significantly upgrade it. You can get a new paint job, throw in a new engine, change out the interior, etc. You can make what you were given the best version possible through your hard work.

Likewise, you could have a Ferrari. But if you want to pour sugar in the gas tank, take a hammer to the engine block, and leave it out in a hail storm, you can ruin what was handed down to you pretty quickly.

I say all of this for two reasons. First, you have to know and believe that you can make significant changes through the work you put in today, no matter what genes you have. Second, your brain is in control of way more than you may realize.

Your unconscious brain is a magnificent creation, much like a thoroughbred racehorse. You, the one reading this book, are simply the conscious mind—the jockey controlling what little you can to affect the outcome.

So how can we be more intentional about this? How can we become better jockeys for our brains?

DISCOUNTING THE SOFT STUFF

How much do you discount the power of the mind?

We all "know" the mind is a powerful thing, but do you believe it? If you genuinely believe it, do you have some mental training program you follow? Do you have a regular practice of positive self-talk and visualization?

If not, then why not?

As Andrew Carnegie said, "As I grow older, I pay less attention to what men say. I watch what they do."

I don't find many who will say they don't believe the mind is a powerful thing. Most will fully agree with this fact. However, I very rarely run into someone who is trying to harness and train that potential power.

Why? Because it's uncomfortable.

It's not only uncomfortable to start a daily practice like this, but it will also come with push-back and skepticism proffered by yourself and society.

In short: People will think you are weird. Hell, you may think you are weird.

But is it that weird?

THE MOST IMPORTANT PICTURE

Let me open the can of worms on weird for you.

If you are an entrepreneur long enough, or at all, really, you will, at some point, be introduced to the work of Napoleon Hill and the book, *Think and Grow Rich.*

An idea introduced in the book is what some people refer to as the Law of Attraction. Here is the definition of the Law of Attraction from Wikipedia and forgive the Wikipedia reference. Still, when you get a little woo-woo, there aren't a lot of places to turn to for sources. Here is the definition, or idea:

> "The Law of Attraction is the belief that positive or negative thoughts bring positive or negative experiences into a person's life. The belief-based on the idea that people and their thoughts are both made from pure energy. Through the process of like energy attracting

like energy, a person can improve their
health, wealth, and personal relationships."

Now, this isn't the same thing as thinking positive
thoughts to be optimistic. The true zealots of the Law
of Attraction believe you can sit in your living room,
concentrate on $1,000,000, and it will appear in your
bank account.

In my experience, there are three ways people use
this information.

- Route 1: Complete disregard it as cooky and
  move on.
- Route 2: Completely embrace the idea and
  believe that just thinking positive thoughts
  will give you everything you want.
- Route 3: Take the middle ground by thinking
  the positive thoughts but backing it up with
  an absurd amount of hard work.

Honestly, I've known people who have taken every
route but, I see the most results from those who
embrace the third route. Go figure.

But, as you may have gleaned from my chapter on
letting go of ideas, it's kind of tough for me to latch
on to new things right away, especially something like
this.

However, I also know a meta-analysis of 13 studies
with a total of 370 participants exists, showing,
conclusively, that motor imagery training alone
enhances strength compared to doing nothing.

The first study I ever read on these topics was by The
Department of Biomedical Engineering at the Lerner

Research Institute, which also showed that mental power relates to muscle power.

Here is the rundown of their study:

- Tested the finger abductor muscles and elbow flexor muscles through 12 weeks of training, five days a week, 15 minutes per day.
- Three groups: Group 1 - Only physical exercise. Group 2 - Control group (did nothing). Group 3 - Only mental exercises.
- Results: Group 1 - 53% increase in strength in each muscle group. Group 2 - No significant change. Group 3 - 35% and 13.5% increase in strength, respectively.

When I first read the study, I thought there would be, maybe, a 5% change, but a 35% increase in strength, just from thinking!? That is impressive.

Now that I know it's scientific fact that you can sit, do nothing, and increase your strength to some degree, what else is possible?

So I dug a little deeper on this Law of Attraction woo-woo idea. While I didn't find any proof that one can manifest things purely by thinking them, I did find the Reticular Activating System (RAS).

From the top of the spinal column to the base of your brain, lives your RAS. All of your senses (except smell) are wired directly to this bundle of neurons. And the RAS is only about the size of your little finger.

The RAS is your brain's filter. Consider this: you're walking into a crowded restaurant to meet your friends for dinner. You walk in, you can't spot your friends, and immediately get hit with an absurd amount of data inputs to your brain. There are a hundred different conversations, the bartender shaking a martini, background music, and more. Your brain is aware of everything that is going on, but if it were to send all that to your conscious mind, you'd end up in an insane asylum. Then, out of nowhere, you hear one of your friends call your name. How is that possible?

Your brain knew to filter and to categorize the background noise, so when it heard your name, it let that through as something known and vital. This filtering is not entirely different from getting a new car and then observing how many other people drive the same one.

So is there a benefit to sitting and thinking about the things you want every single day?

Is it so far-fetched to believe? Whether you are chasing financial goals or physical goals, the more you think about them, the more known and valuable they become to your brain.

Over time, you start to see opportunities—things that might have always been there but that you never noticed because your brain didn't know you cared to see that information.

Perhaps you want to get out of debt, so you start thinking about this goal every day. Then, one day, you are at a friend's house, and you notice a book on their bookshelf about getting out of debt. To you, it may seem serendipitous, but to your brain, it's merely letting in what you are focusing on.

There isn't a concrete way to visualize your goals. Still, from what scientific data can be collected from tangible results using mental visualization, the approach is for participants to imagine themselves performing each exercise.

Specifically, looking out through their own eyes (i.e., a first-person view), and maximally exerting themselves through the exercise.

Can you imagine yourself, in the first-person, achieving a goal you want?

You may want to start forming that picture today; it may be the most compelling picture you've ever created. Do it, and your brain may begin to perceive things a little bit differently.

After you have that in your mind, we can talk about it to ourselves.

THE MOST IMPORTANT CONVERSATION

Let me point out to you a commonly ignored fact: you talk to yourself. You talk to yourself constantly.

In fact, after having read the previous sentence, you most likely had some internal dialogue about talking to yourself. Studies have revealed that we speak to ourselves somewhere at a rate of between 300 to 1000 words every single minute. Other studies conclude our rate of inner speech can average 4,000 words per minute—10 times faster than verbal expression.

What can we do with this incredible amount of internal chatter?

In a 2017 study, two groups of high-level kickboxers performed the same lifting program over 12 weeks. One group completed only physical training, while the other group did the same exercise with additional mental training, including motivational self-talk.

Across the board, the results were quite phenomenal. The physical plus mental training group outperformed the physical only group in every category. In many cases, the improvement from baseline physical testing percentage was double that of the group who did only physical training.

Further, the physical plus mental training group's testosterone levels were higher, cortisol levels were lower, blood pressure was lower, and had resting heart rates which were significantly improved compared to the physical only training group.

It turns out that the conversation you are having with yourself right now is pretty important. So how do we control the conversation?

Here's how they trained the participants in this study:

The motivational self-talk was self-selected, so each individual wasn't given a list of 10 affirmations to start with as their "self-talk." You know, what many self-help gurus out there would have you start doing. It was more simplistic.

The athletes were told to identify negative self-talk before, during, or after training, write down the negative statement, and to restate that negative statement as a positive or motivating statement.

For example, if an athlete caught himself thinking, "I'm not sure I can lift this much weight," they'd instead be instructed to repeat something like, "I could lift more weight" between sets. The athletes were asked to change their motivational statements each time a new piece of negative self-talk arose.

Pretty easy, right? Why not make the incessant self-talk positive and constructive? Why not become aware of the negative and purposefully turn it around? Why not, instead of allowing thoughts to come and go, proactively think and talk to yourself in the way you want?

It all begins with the structures in the brain, much like the RAS mentioned earlier. In your brain, you have the amygdala. The amygdala is the structure in the brain most associated with fear. When you are afraid, you are likely to have worried thoughts, physical sensations like a faster heart rate, sweating, increased respiratory rate, and other behaviors. For instance, you may be trying to escape the situation that made you afraid in the first place!

Interestingly, recent studies have shown that humans, in general, are very optimistic creatures. Even if you aren't an optimistic person, it doesn't mean you aren't an optimist in some way. A small part of you is hoping for that better future. You work a job you don't like for a salary you wish was higher, and you believe deep down, you will, someday, get the more relaxed, higher-paying job.

Or you work out in a belief that there is a better version of yourself on the other side of all the pain and sweat. If you didn't believe this, you wouldn't do it.

This constant optimism about the future-self has proven to be incredibly powerful. When you think of positive future experiences, things not yet achieved but things that you KNOW you will realize, i.e., a goal, your brain operates at a different level of optimism.

Why does this matter?

This new level of optimism helps the amygdala to downplay negative emotional responses. Now, you are taking a substantial amount of fear and anxiety out of any situation. With apprehension decreased, your mental focus can now increase.

All this gets done with a little positive self-talk.

Allow me to be more succinct. Positive self-talk (mental) has a direct effect on the amygdala (physiological). You are doing way more than pumping yourself up in the mirror before a big presentation. Instead, you are radically reducing physiological responses that hinder performance.

PUTTING IT ALL TOGETHER

I do not feel Navy SEALs deserve greater recognition than any other sailor, soldier, marine, or airman. This said, they do undergo what may be the most rigorous mental and physical training programs the U.S. Military has to offer with one of the highest attrition rates.

But what many people don't understand is that any person who goes to SEAL training these days is a very highly qualified candidate. The Navy doesn't pride themselves on failing candidates out of Basic Underwater Demolition/SEAL (BUD/S) training, moreso it's not cost-effective to do so.

To retain more of these high-powered individuals, and figure out what makes the successful candidates successful, the Navy conducted an extensive study. They published the results in a paper detailing the predictors of success in Basic Underwater Demolition/SEAL Training.

Here are the three most important determinants of success:

1. level of physical fitness
2. psychological skills such as self-talk and visualization
3. arousal control, i.e., getting that amygdala in check

Not surprisingly, when the Navy started introducing more mental training into their program, the pass rate increased from 25% to 33%, according to Dr. Akil professor at Florida State University. This is an enormous increase for one of the most grueling physical training programs in the world.

It seems to me, that if hardcore Navy SEALs go on a mental training program, then you should too. And it's not that hard to accomplish.

TAKEAWAYS

1. **Brainpower.** Brain power gets thrown to the curb, yet, it may be your most potent weapon.
2. **Visualization.**Visualization is practical and scientific, not woo-woo.
3. **Self-Talk.**You talk to yourself a lot. Control that self-talk as much as you can.
4. **Start Your Program.** Like any successful training program two things need to happen. First, you need to start. Second, you need to stick with it.

9. LEADERSHIP

"Do not follow where the path may lead. Go instead, where there is no path and leave a trail." **Ralph Waldo Emerson**

Mastering leadership is a Sisyphean effort.

There are no formulas. There are no concrete answers. In leadership, there are always unclear pathways, shades of gray, dichotomies, imperfection. Leading is one of the most uncomfortable things a human can do.

But, it is not leadership itself, nor is it the act of trying to master leadership that makes for our final trap of comfort.

Given: inaction is more comfortable to accomplish. Even though we are all given ample opportunities to lead ourselves and others, we opt out too often and inaction is a slippery slope.

Napoleon Bonaparte said, "A revolution can be neither made nor stopped. The only thing that can be done is for one of several of its children to give it a direction by dint of victories."

When we lead, we shape our futures through a dint of victory. Failure to lead comes from a desire to remain comfortable, and it shapes society through a lack of victory.

THE TROPHY THAT RUINED A GENERATION

A 2014 Reason-Rupe survey found that a substantial majority of Americans (57 %) said only winners should get a trophy. Furthermore, 40% believe all kids on a sports team should receive a prize for their participation, also known as a participation trophy.

A participation trophy is a trophy a kid gets for simply having participated in a sport or activity. They don't have to win or excel; they just have to show up and participate.

There are popular theories and ideas about how participation trophies have ruined an entire generation because that's "not how real life works."

Today, there are parents ripping trophies from their kid's hands and returning them. I've heard fathers proudly state, "there are no participation trophies in this house." As if they have figured out what it takes to make their kid an ideal citizen who does not possess the undesirable trait of entitlement.

The idea is that if every kid gets a trophy without winning anything, we are teaching them to think they should be heavily celebrated simply for showing up. So, are we to instead, teach them that the only path worth pursuing in this life is to win? Or, as Ricky Bobby put it, "If you ain't first, you're last."

WHAT'S OLD IS NEW: THE PROBLEM

To point the finger at a trophy is to take a myopic view and forget history.

History shows that laziness and entitlement are not new struggles for humans.

It's why in his inaugural address, John F. Kennedy said, "Ask not what your country can do for you, ask what you can do for your country."

Andrew Carnegie, who poured himself into educating young men about how to set off on the path to success said, "It is not the poor young man who goes forth to his work in the morning and labours until evening that we should pity. It is the son of the rich man who cannot be trusted with this honourable task."

To quote Ralph Waldo Emerson, who wrote sincerely on this topic in his essay *The Law of Compensation,* "Who doth not work shall not eat."

As early as 1922, high school students in Columbus, Ohio were awarded participation trophies for merely showing up at a basketball tournament. This was not a one-time incident, as events like this one have occurred many times over the last 100 years.

Human behavior is human behavior and, in a thousand years from today, we still will not have it figured out.

To believe that one single, childhood event , such as the receiving of a participation trophy, could lead to such widespread problems is ludicrous. Wouldn't it be awesome if we could so easily attribute cause and effect to human behavior? I wish we could. If cause and effect were that obvious, then correcting our behavior would be easy.

The truth is that being rewarded for participation is exactly how real life works.

Are you currently collecting a paycheck from somewhere and aren't number one in sales, in production, or whatever? Aren't you still showing up every day and putting in the work and providing value? This is what matters.

Are you working out every day but not winning a gold medal in the Olympics or, in a less dramatic example, do you run, but aren't coming in first place in your local 5K race? Is participating in an activity without trying to place first, OK?

If your kids, or those around you, see you work out every day, you are teaching the lesson that if you show up every day and put in the work, you get results.

We don't have a trophy problem—we have a perception problem.

THE FIX

Dr. Carol Dweck, professor of Psychology at Stanford University and author of the book Mindset, has done the most in-depth research on what praise can do to a child.

In an analysis published in the Journal of Personality and Social Psychology, Dweck and her colleagues reviewed six studies which looked at different types of praise and how each affects a child's willingness to perform and take on challenges.

Contrary to popular belief, these six studies demonstrated that praise for an innate ability like intelligence had more negative consequences for students' achievement motivation than recognition for effort.

In other words, when you only focus on the outcome (winning) and you don't attribute that to the process (participation), children develop what Dweck refers to as a "fixed" mindset over a "growth" mindset.

Her research suggests that if we want children to improve in any area, we need to reward effort, not only talent and not only achievement (the trophy). Participation trophies can be an essential part of this approach.

I have three kids, two of whom are old enough to play organized sports. Both of them have already received participation trophies. When they get the award, I briefly explain they got that trophy for making it to every practice, showing up to every game, and trying their hardest in the process. That is the lesson I will teach them. They participated and got rewarded, they were consistent, they put in the work, and they tried hard. They can now detach themselves from the outcome and only focus on the process.

Epictetus put it this way, "Some things are within our power, while others are not. Within our power are opinion, motivation, desire, aversion, and, in a word, whatever is of our own doing; not within our power are our body, our property, reputation, office, and, in a word, whatever is not of our own doing."

Set goals, focus on the process, and detach from what's outside of your control.

As Dweck suggests, I must instill in my children a growth mindset, and this is no easy task for any parent.

Alternatively, I could rip the trophy from their hands and say, "You didn't earn that!!"? I am no psychologist, but I venture to guess that if I were to do so, my kids wouldn't respect me, nor would they remember the incident fondly as grown-ups.

John Maxwell once said, "The pessimist complains about the wind. The optimist expects it to change. The leader adjusts the sails."

Do you want to complain about the problem? Do you want to wish and hope the problem resolves on its own? Or, do you want to make the adjustment needed to navigate your current environment?

If you are leaning towards option 3, you are ready to lead.

Leadership is how we influence, or even change, human behavior. Pointing at problems is the antithesis of leadership.

Leading is always the more uncomfortable choice.

So, where does leadership start?

9. LEADERSHIP

SELF LEADERSHIP

The Isthmian games, organized by the city of Corinth in ancient Greece were second in fame only to the Olympic Games. In a letter to these Corinthians, the apostle Paul wrote,

"So I do not run aimlessly; I do not box as one beating the air. But I discipline my body and keep it under control, lest after preaching to others I myself should be disqualified."

Paul frequently used athletic metaphors to describe the rigors and single-minded focus of his work. He also illustrates perfectly where leadership begins.

First, you have to know you are a leader. If you only lead yourself—you are a leader, even if you don't feel like a leader.

Van Gogh once said, "If you hear a voice within you say you cannot paint, then by all means, paint and that voice will be silenced."

If you feel you are not a leader, the best response is to lead.

And, as a leader, if you cannot maintain self-discipline and keep yourself under control, why would you be worth listening to?

Like you are instructed to do when the oxygen mask falls from above in the airplane during a loss of cabin pressure, put your mask on first.

The act of taking care of yourself first isn't self-centeredness, it's self-leadership. Leading yourself is the prerequisite to success.

And that is where you have to begin. Mastering the self.

TAKEAWAYS

1. **Blame is Easy, Fixing is Hard.** Problems are easy to spot, the catalyst is difficult to uncover, and the resolution—the hardest of all.
2. **Leadership is the Answer.** If the problem involves human behavior, leadership is the answer.
3. **Lead Yourself First.** Leadership starts with you.

PART 2: THE TRUTH

AVIATE

NAVIGATE

COMMUNICATE

AVIATE - NAVIGATE - COMMUNICATE

While I was a pilot trainee, one thing the instructors taught us was Aviate - Navigate - Communicate. It's one of the most basic and vital principles in aviation.

When an inexperienced pilot gets into trouble, the natural tendency is to do things a little out of order, i.e., radio in to tell someone about the situation and next, try to figure out their position in order to assess potential emergency landing locations. All good things to be doing until the pilot realizes he may not be focusing on flying the airplane, which is what will most certainly keep him alive.

It is an elementary principle, and it suggests the *"what's the closest alligator to the boat"* metaphor/question. Meaning, it doesn't matter if you have 50 problems or "alligators" about to take out your boat, you only need to focus on the single closest and most pressing alligator (issue). Once that issue is resolved, you can move to the next.

Our lives are not that different. When we know we require a change, we buy a program, start a diet, or set a goal—most of which we don't stick to and, eventually, we fail. We fail because we are not addressing our problems in the right order.

To start killing comfort, you have to take honest stock of where you currently are. And that's what we will be covering in Part 2 of this book, the Aviate - Navigate - Communicate process and how it applies to your life. Let's start with a brief introduction to each concept.

AVIATE

In December 1972, Flight 401, flying over Florida, had a malfunction that was demanding the attention of four professional aviators. The landing gear position indicator light was incorrect. The entire crew was single-mindedly focused on this malfunction.

Unfortunately, no one was left to focus on keeping the plane in the air as it headed into a shallow descent towards the Florida Everglades. The crew was so focused on a non-critical task that they failed to detect and arrest the descent of the aircraft. This failure to focus on the very basics of aviation resulted in 99 fatalities. The aviators were unable to first fly the plane.

In life, we are the airplane, and we need to start focusing on flying it a little bit better before we do anything else.

Goal-setting is excellent, but to be honest, it is highly ineffective. I don't care if you are writing down goals or getting them tattooed on your forehead. You can't start achieving goals until you take control of yourself.

You need to prove to yourself that you can take action, daily action, something outside of your routine, and you need to do it every day without fail. It doesn't matter if it's a breathing practice, working out, walking, or eating a vegetable. Choose something that's not normal for you, and do it every day, for a long time. In this way you develop the habit of action.

How is this different from goal-setting?

Goals and planning bring the future into the present.

Daily micro actions focus only on the present. These are small habits you know you should be doing. This is about what you are doing today and only today, with no focus on tomorrow or where it will lead. It's a practice of action.

NAVIGATE

After you can aviate, figuring out where you are and where you're going is pretty important.

To "navigate," we bring your future into the present and set a goal (not goals). I am not talking about traditional goal-setting. I am talking about a type of single-minded goal-setting that when implemented correctly, cannot fail.

Most people want to start with "navigate." People want to make a dreamboard, work on visualizations, repeat daily affirmations, and set big goals.

People start here because it is the most fun. It's fun to envision our futures and make plans, but I am going to tell you something that challenges that idea.

First, you must develop the habit of action, or "aviate" before moving to "navigate." Anything that you want to go after, any goal that you have, any goal that's worth achieving, worth doing, is going to take daily action over decades. You need to prove to yourself that you're the type of person who can do something every day.

COMMUNICATE

Communication is simple.

In aviation, it's talking to air traffic control or someone outside the airplane (Communicate).

In our lives, it's accountability. It's about being part of a tribe, one that understands your situation and encourages your next steps. It's telling your friends and family about your journey and about inspiring others.

Developing a habit of action and setting a singular focus are prerequisites to the "communicate" phase. Otherwise, you'll be the person who watches a documentary, gets all fired up to make a change, and maybe even tells some friends. However, if you aren't the type of person who can keep a commitment, you are instead the boy who cried wolf. You are simply telling everyone your new flavor of the week, and they know it.

In "aviate" and "navigate," you learn to *do* first and then to commit. You become the person who does what you say you're going to do and follows through. If you think people forget about your commitments, they don't. They are just too nice to tell you they noticed. Next, they hold you to a lesser standard.

96

Inaction is a slippery slope. Never communicate too early.

10. AVIATE

 **"Hard choices, easy life. Easy choices, hard life."** Jerzy Gregorek

For years, I have obsessed over my performance and the idea of mental toughness.

It was 2014, when I was at a neuromuscular research laboratory taking part in human warrior performance testing and research (run by the University of Pittsburgh), when I came to the realization my approach to training may be a little unique.

My head was pounding and it was hard to catch my breath.

I was pedaling on a bike, trying to concentrate on the fact that I still needed to keep moving, even though the test was over. I felt a pain creeping up into my neck and the back of my head—great, an exercise-induced headache (EIH)...I'd experienced an EIH only one other time, and it was awful.

Trying not to focus on the pain, I couldn't help but look up at the research assistants staring blankly at me. They turned, pressed a few more buttons on their computers, and glanced at a "leaderboard" they had created for all of the physical fitness tests. Finally, they spoke. "You just broke three records..."

They asked, "What workouts do you do?" "Who do you train with?"

One of my good friends and training partners was also there for the test and he just started laughing. He answered for me since I was still out of breath. "He pretty much trains alone...in his garage...with a barbell."

Rewind to a few months earlier, and I'm sitting at Chili's with about a dozen special operations airmen, discussing hard physical challenges. I had just ordered an avocado bacon burger when I realized this cold, hard fact: I had just committed to running a marathon with less than 72 hours to prepare. I hadn't run more than one mile at a time in the last year...was this a good idea?

Three days later, there I was, running a marathon on a quarter-mile track. It was lap 82 of 105 when I decided it would be a good idea to try and run backward for a quarter-mile to try and ease a little bit of the pain in my hips and knees. As I transitioned to running backward, I felt a ridiculous pain when merely turning my body around. Yep, this was a bad idea but I couldn't quit, I was on track to run the marathon a full hour faster than I had expected.

Fast forward a few months past the human performance testing, to max out day. I was on a ridiculous quest to lift one million pounds by counting only the volume in three lifts: squat, press, and deadlift. I was standing at the bar, ready to attempt a triple bodyweight deadlift. I had just maxed out on squat and press and set new personal records. I had even failed twice already at two other more substantial squat attempts. Before I addressed the bar,

10. AVIATE

I was simply thinking how lucky I was that I didn't get crushed by the bar on my failed squat attempt. As my mind started to wander, my buddy clapped his hands and said, "Let's go!" I cleared my head, grabbed the bar, and achieved a long-time goal—a triple bodyweight deadlift.

That next year, I was on a quest to complete a 100-mile single-day bike race in August, in Texas, on a 30-plus-pound, steel-framed, single-speed bike wearing a 10-plus-pound pack.

I was on mile 84 of 100 with no prior cycling training when my self-talk got very interesting.

At mile 70, I decided to stop and see if I could find some sunscreen. I went to the medical tent, and the medics slapped a can of SPF 50 spray on sunscreen onto the table. I reached my left hand out to grab the canister and knocked it right over, which got me some funny looks from the medical staff. I immediately realized I no longer had the use of my left hand. Fearing the medical team would try and get me to stop the race, I picked up the bottle with my good hand and walked away.

I finished the race, albeit painfully and slowly, but I finished.

I do stuff like this for one reason: Mental Toughness Practice.

These events and the pursuit of personal performance are not attempts to be the best in the world. Instead, I am aiming to set new individual mental benchmarks.

I had achieved a lot as an athlete and felt I was building mental toughness, but something was missing in the translation. Just completing one hard event or one hard training program wasn't transforming who I was in my daily life.

I wanted to pursue hard things, but I also wanted this pursuit to make me fully show up as a father and husband. I want it to make me a better business owner, a better human.

That's when I came up with the "Hard Things Equation."

THE HARD THINGS EQUATION

I have had the opportunity to interview hundreds of elite performers, special operators, fighter pilots, world-renowned surgeons, PhDs leading their fields in academia, professional athletes, scientists, and more.

One question I asked every single one of them was, "In your opinion, what's the best activity for building mental toughness?"

If I had to boil all of their responses down to one straightforward idea, it would be this: do hard things. Do the things you know you should do, but don't want to do. Doing hard things will force you to embrace discomfort.

What should you do? We could put a rock in your shoe to force you to embrace discomfort with every step, but that would be stupid. I am talking about chasing the type of discomfort that will transform who you are. You get there with the Hard Things Equation.

HARD THINGS EQUATION

$$\text{Pushing Forward Against Your Own Desire} + \text{Daily Over Decades} = \text{Hard Thing}$$

BREAKING DOWN THE EQUATION

Let's break down the equation.

PART ONE: PUSHING FORWARD AGAINST YOUR OWN DESIRE

Newton's First Law of Motion states, an object at rest stays at rest unless acted upon by an outside force. Similarly, an object in motion stays in motion unless...you get the picture.

To do hard things, you will have to force yourself into action every single day. Inaction is comfortable, action is hard.

Interestingly, the more you do hard things, the easier they become. Eventually, you form a habit, and then you become an object in motion, and you will remain in motion unless some outside force acts upon you. I've listed six possible things that would slow you down in Part 1 of this book.

To push forward against your desire doesn't have to be running an impromptu marathon, competing in a

100-mile bike race, or setting a performance record. Pushing forward against your own desire could be something as humble as doing the dishes every single day. It could be going for a walk. It could be taking 17 seconds to breathe and visualize.

The action can be as big or as small as you want it to be. The size of the obstacle you want to push against has everything to do with where you currently are and what you can handle, something we will assess in Part 3, the implementation portion of this book.

In short, if working out every day, eating clean, and being healthy is easy for you—it's time to find the next big thing to push against. If you feel like you are terrible at forming habits or doing anything consistently, you start small...like tiny. You push forward each day against one small obstacle until it is mastered.

PART TWO: DAILY OVER DECADES

The "Daily Over Decades" idea was presented to you in Chapter 3. To summarize, Daily Over Decades is concentrated effort on discomfort every single day over decades.

Being uncomfortable for a moment will yield minimal results. However, discomfort on a long enough timeline will produce serious results.

Going on a walk every day this month...some results.

Going on a walk every day for the rest of your life...mind-blowing improvements in your health and longevity.

10. AVIATE

We live in a world of 6-week challenges and failed New Year's resolutions. When you put something in the perspective of decades, it brings clarity to your actions. It becomes the litmus test for part one of the equation.

If I pressed you this very second to come up with an action you would push forward with, against your own desire, you may select something big and exciting.

You see, people get revved up like this all the time. They've had it, and enough is enough, so today is the day they start working out, change their diet, start waking up early, begin a meditation practice, and even begin journaling—all great things. There's just one problem, they aren't ready to take on ALL those new habits or hard things.

Now, if I pressed you again this very second to come up with an action you will push forward with, against your own desire, with the caveat that you are going to need to do it every day for the next decade, you'd get more realistic. You may set your sights on just one of the actions I mentioned above, or something even smaller.

THE REAL HABIT

If you pick up the habit of walking, it's excellent for your health and that's awesome. But that is not my concern here. What I want for you is to learn how to go on that walk when it's cold and raining, when you've had a bad day, when there is not even an ounce of you that desires to go outside and walk, but you do it anyway. That's the real habit we are developing. Some call it grit, some call it mental toughness, we are calling it a hard thing.

The "decades" portion of the equation helps focus our efforts but does not require perfection. While perfection is great, we are all human and will fall short at some point, so disconnect perfection of achievement with what it is we are doing. I could care less about checkmarks on a habit tracker. We are trying to "aviate" and focus on small hard things we can do in our daily lives each day. These hard things don't need to connect to a bigger goal or an ideal lifestyle. They are simply hard things we practice every day to develop the habit of taking action when we don't want to.

The equation is simple, Pushing Forward Against Your Own Desire + Daily Over Decades = Hard Thing. Over time, the progress is geometric, not linear. I am not suggesting you pick up one habit for a full decade before you can start any other practices or hard things. What you will find is, over time, that one hard thing becomes an easy thing. You are no longer pushed or challenged by it. For some people this takes weeks and for some people, it takes years. But when you get to that point, that is when you can add more hard things to your life.

This mastery over hard things, making them easy, will come more quickly the more things you master.

The hard things equation forces you to find what's next, feasible, and realistic. Once you've done that, you'll discover your real sticking power and finally be able to unleash it.

TAKEAWAYS

1. **Making Success Mathematical.** Use the hard things equation to make a decision. Don't guess.
2. **The Hard Things Equation Power.** The power of the equation is time. Like compounding interest, you pick up steam the more times you use it.
3. **Daily Over Decades, Against Desire.** There are two parts to the equation, you need both.

This idea should set you free and put your mind at ease. A list of a hundred things you'll never stick to will never beat a list of one thing you'll always do.

Bruce Lee put it this way, "I fear not the man who has practiced 10,000 kicks once, but I fear the man who has practiced one kick 10,000 times."

11. NAVIGATE

"The man who chases two rabbits, catches neither." Confucius

On January 15, 2009, things got dicey quickly after US Airways Flight 1549 took off from New York City's LaGuardia Airport. Aboard the airplane were 150 passengers and five crew members, including pilot Chesley Sullenberger, all bound for Charlotte, NC, when...

Sullenberger: "Hit birds. We've lost thrust on both engines. We're turning back towards LaGuardia."

LaGuardia departure control: ok, uh, you need to return to LaGuardia? Turn left heading of uh two two zero.

Departure control: Cactus fifteen twenty nine, if we can get it for you do you want to try to land runway one three?

Sullenberger: We're unable. We may end up in the Hudson.

Departure control: Alright Cactus fifteen forty-nine it's going to be left traffic for runway three-one.

Sullenberger: Unable.

Departure Control: Ok, what do you need to land?

...8 seconds of deafening silence...

11. NAVIGATE

Departure control: Cactus fifteen [twenty] nine runway four's available if you want to make left traffic to runway four.

Sullenberger: I'm not sure we can make any runway. Uh, what's over to our right anything in New Jersey, maybe Teterboro?

Departure control: You wanna try and go to Teterboro?

Sullenberger: Yes.

Departure control: Cactus fifteen twenty nine turn right two eight zero, you can land runway one at Teterboro.

Sullenberger: We can't do it.

Departure control: 'Kay which runway would you like at Teterboro?

Sullenberger: We're going to be in the Hudson.

Departure control (15:29:33): I'm sorry, say again, Cactus?

Three minutes into the flight, the aircraft struck a flock of Canada geese and lost power in both engines. Air traffic controllers tried to divert the US Airways plane back to LaGuardia or to a nearby airport in New Jersey. Captain Chesley "Sully" Sullenberger decided he could not safely land the aircraft in either of the airports, instructed passengers to "brace for impact," and glided the plane into the Hudson River.

There's nothing more Captain Sully wanted that day than to take 150 passengers to Charlotte, NC. After the bird strike, Captain Sully's greatest desire was to land safely on a paved runway. However, the plane ended up in the Hudson River. Things didn't go as planned, and a Hudson-River landing was more like plan E after, A, B, C, and D failed.

When we set goals, we often get in the all-or-nothing mentality. Any new habit you are trying to build, you expect perfection. Then, one day, you fail on your diet, you skip a workout, you miss your goal. Unlike Sully, however, we don't navigate to our alternate possibilities. Often, we throw our hands in the air and call it quits.

This is true in the goals we set for ourselves but not in other areas of our life. On any given day, if I could have lead or parented my children better, but I fail to, I don't relinquish my responsibilities as a father and say, "Screw it, I am not doing this anymore." I recalibrate, reassess, and re engage the next day. Similarly, if you are late to work one day, do you quit your job because you are now shy of perfection? Of course not. However, in a quest for self-development, this is the approach many take.

Perfection is impossible. When we drop the all-or-nothing mentality and embrace the bumps in the road, we are free to accomplish anything we set our minds to do.

FINDING ATOM

When I started my company, I did a 15-minute call with every athlete who signed up for our service until I could no longer keep up. I did over 1,000 one-on-one calls with athletes to figure out who they were, what they needed, and how I could help them.

One question I asked all of them was, "What is your goal?"

Most of the time, people responded with something very vague and non-specific. Very rarely was someone able to tell me about a precise, well-defined goal.

Over time, I developed a process called "Finding Atom" to drag a goal out of those I would talk to. As you know, an atom is the smallest unit of an element. You have to dig deep to find it and it also holds tremendous power. This "atom" would be the one thing I would have the athlete work on. No list of things. One singular thing, their atom.

This process worked so well that I began to use it in my business consulting work, my personal life, and continued to use it with my athletes.

Goal setting is the hardest thing for people to do, but **Finding Atom** is not goal-setting. It's finding where you are and where you need to be; it's the "Navigate" in our Aviate - Navigate - Communicate process.

CURRENT LOCATION

First, we find where you are to see what's possible and where you can go from there. In Sully's second radio communication to departure control, he said, "We may end up in the Hudson." He took stock of where he was and realized what was possible for him at that moment.

An easy way to do this is to find where you are comfortable. Comfort is like a slow-growing cancer, and I've seen take over the lives of many people. No one decides, "I wanna be lazy and gain weight." It happens gradually over years. You just get a little bit more comfortable, a little bit more complacent.

So let's start there, but a caveat before we do. I do not believe that you always have to be chasing more. Everyone can improve, but the never-ending hamster wheel of more will only lead to bankruptcy and unhappiness. We are looking for areas of your life where you've unknowingly gotten complacent and don't desire to be that way. This process is like shining a flashlight on areas of your life you would like to improve.

Discomfort is a sign of progress. Where are you most comfortable right now? Are there any areas of your life where you don't feel that you're being pushed or challenged? Comfort in any area is an excellent indicator that you are not growing, and that you have plateaued. But first, we need to find out if you are complacent or, perhaps, you are simply content.

WHERE YOU WANT TO GO: CONTENT OR COMPLACENT

Here are the places we will start looking: your finances, your spiritual life, your health, your relationships, your business, your work, your personal life.

For each of the areas listed above, do a quick mental assessment of where you are and decide if you are content or complacent.

Content means you are currently satisfied with where you are in an area. For example, in your finances, there is always the "more/hamster wheel" you could hop on. However, say you like what you earn, save, and give and you love the life you live. If so, you are content with your financial situation, and that's ok. However, if you know you have more drive and ambition that is not being put to good use and it could equate to a better financial situation for you and your family, then you would be complacent.

Take a few minutes to walk through the Content or Complacent Exercise. If you are like most, you may have more than one area in which you are complacent, and that's ok. You now need to pick one and only one area that you would like to improve.

Congrats, we've found Atom! Now, we can aim for where we would like to go through the AMP process, Aim - Motivation - Purpose.

AIM, MOTIVATION, AND PURPOSE (AMP)

One day my son got a toy tank that fires tiny plastic missiles, and it wasn't long before we were competing to launch the tiny missiles the farthest.

At first, I crushed him due to the simple fact that I understood trajectory and he didn't. The basic idea behind trajectory is not to aim too high nor too low when you are trying to maximize the distance covered. The goal is to aim somewhere in the middle.

After I gave him a 2-minute lesson, he got the idea, and it was an even playing field. Trajectory relates one hundred percent to how you should be setting goals.

After you can "aviate," goal-setting becomes your "navigate." Now, we bring the future into the present and decide where we want to go. But before we decide, let's jump back to the trajectory.

I'm sure you've heard things like "you gotta think BIG" when people are talking about goals, but I say yes, and no.

Here's how trajectory works.

If you set a REALLY BIG unrealistic goal, you are going to aim high, then launch. You will go out soaring, only to find out things are hard, and you will come down almost on the same path you went up. So, in actual distance covered, you didn't make it very far. If you aim too low, you won't cover much distance either. Low goals = low achievement. But if you set the most realistic and achievable goal and aim "just right." You will cover the most distance and make the most progress.

Feel free to think big and have the big goal. But don't put it in your crosshairs yet. What you need to put in your crosshairs is the next and most logical thing you can achieve. If an F-15 wants to fly across the Atlantic, it's going to take multiple meetings with a tanker to refuel...miss even one of those meetings on the way, and it will never make it.

Keep an eye on that big goal as a target you'll get to, but don't aim for it immediately. First, chase what you can achieve and use achievements as stepping stones.

If you come right out of the gate with the most significant goal imaginable, what happens if you don't achieve it in 6 to 12 months?? You'll feel defeated. You'll lose momentum. All you need to succeed is to keep moving forward. To keep that momentum, you need the right trajectory.

So, let's take aim and start the AMP process. Know that the AMP process can be done for each area of your life, work, health, spirituality, etc.

AIM

Take the one area you have selected and aim high but also a decade out. We aren't putting anything in stone here. Simply imagine for a brief moment what this area of your life could look like in 10 years. Specifically, I want you to imagine two things. First, what does this area of your life look like if you do nothing and keep doing what you are doing? Second, what does this area look like if you were to give it some attention daily over the next decade? We cannot focus on our next steps until we know where we are going. After you have your 10-year picture, what's the one thing you have to do in the next five years to be on track to achieve your 10-year goal? After you have your 5-year target, what's the one thing you have to do in the next year to be on track to achieve your 5-year goal? Reverse engineer your success one step at a time.

Once you have that picture in your head, I have to ask, "Why?"

MOTIVATION

I'm going to ask you, or instead, you'll be asking yourself, "Why?" five times. I'll walk you through an example, then you can do this on your own. When I started my business, I wanted it to be financially successful. Since finances were a significant point of stress for my family and me when I first started, it was a primary goal to have it be able to support my family. Here's what asking "why" five times turned into for me.

Goal: I want a financially successful business.

Why do I want to do this?

- *It will give me more freedom, options, choices, and provide less stress over money.*

Why do I want to do this (freedom and less stress)?

- *I want more options and less stress because I will be able to provide a pretty epic life for my kids, Emily and myself well into the later stages of life. Less stressed is also the best version of me and Emily.*

Why do I want to do this (epic life & best version)?

- *I love my family more than anything else, and I never want to hold them back from seeing more, being more, or achieving more. Nor do I want to hold them back by being a lesser version of myself (anxious, stressed, preoccupied).*

Why do I want to do this (empower the future of your family)?

- *I am both the strongest and weakest link in my family. I want to prove that I can provide an amazing life for everyone in my family.*

Why do I want to do this (proof)?

- *Maybe because it's never been done in my family. I feel a strong desire to be the best, build an empire, leave a legacy, and take care of the humans in my life better than anyone else can.*

When the "why" gets bigger and bigger, the "how" gets easier and easier. So feel free to take this as big as you want to! When you have a gigantic "why," there will be nothing stopping you when it comes to getting things done. You will learn what you have to learn, you will do what you have to do, and you will do it as long as it takes to succeed. This is not true of a small unemotional "why." Get to the real root of why you are doing what you are doing.

Personally, five layers deep, and I now have a mission statement for my life:

Be the Best.

Build an Empire.

Leave a Legacy.

PURPOSE

Here's a quick recap of where we are in the AMP process:

A - In the AIM portion, you look ahead and reverse engineer where your crosshairs should be for the next step. Now, you know where you are going.

M - Next, you go deep on your motivation and answer "why" 5 times to get to the real motivation for why you are doing what you are doing.

Now, on to the P. What is your purpose? Your aim tells you what to do next, your motivation keeps you fired up and focused, and your purpose will pull you through when things get tough.

All I want you to do, for now, is take a shot at articulating your purpose. That's it. Don't put this task on a pedestal. It can be changed, refined, and perfected over time. Later in the book, there is an entire chapter dedicated to the illustration of a purpose or a "one thing."

But right now, you have all the raw materials. You know where you want to go in the big picture and you even the next steps. You also understand why you are motivated to achieve this one thing. Now, through the lens of that knowledge, what do you feel your purpose is?

You may have never attempted to do something like this, but now is the time.

TAKEAWAYS

1. **Proper Aim In the NEXT Step.** For your immediate next step, don't aim too high. Don't aim too low. Aim somewhere in the middle and succeed. Do it over and over and over again, and that is the exact formula for that big goal even standing a chance of coming to fruition.
2. **Why?** Ask yourself, "why?" five times to uncover your real motivation.
3. **Your Purpose.** Take a shot at articulating your purpose. It may not be as hard as you think.

12. COMMUNICATE

"If your actions inspire others to dream more, learn more, do more and become more, you are a leader." John Quincy Adams

A 2010 meta-analysis spanning 148 studies and 308,849 participants took a look at everything from breathing cleaner air to flu vaccination as weighted factors that influence our risk for mortality.

And what beats out fresh air, body composition, use of alcohol/tobacco, and even our physical fitness? It is our interaction with other humans, specifically, our close relationships and social integration. Basically, how we interact with other people in our day-to-day lives is the single most powerful influence on our mortality.

You can restrict your calories, you can exercise twice a day, and you can load up on kale, but if you lack the human side to this being human thing, the outlook isn't so great.

And that's why we bring other humans into the last part of our aviate, navigate, and communicate process.

12. COMMUNICATE

ALWAYS SOUND COOL

The unwritten first rule of radio communication in the U.S. Military that spans from fighter pilots to green berets is, "Always Sound Cool."

It doesn't matter if you are bored out of your mind or watching bullets whiz past you, when you key that mic, you better sound damn cool, calm, and collected.

So far in our process, we have gotten you to "aviate." You've worked on the blocking and tackling in your daily life. Doing the simple and hard things in the present moment that can alter who you are.

Next, we got you to "navigate." We figured out where you are and where you need to go. Now, we move to "communicate" where we involve others in our journey. These steps are sequential, and you can't move from one to the next until the previous has been mastered. If you do them out of order, you won't sound cool.

We will get to exactly what and how to communicate, but first, here are the three most common errors in the communication phase:

1. Communicating Too Early
2. Communicating in Fragments
3. Communicating Excitement

First, don't start communicating with your friends and family before you have proven you are the type of person who can take action (Aviate) and stick to those actions.

Second, don't start communicating half ideas or things that you could do or should do. Only communicate what you will do and do so with extreme clarity.

Third, don't get all excited about some new plan you have and start telling everyone about it. Wait 'til the excitement fades, then decide if you are still going to press forward. If you are still in it after the initial excitement that's a good sign and now communication can begin.

COMMUNICATE

There are two forms of communication in this phase, internal and external.

Earlier in the book, I discussed self-talk and pointed to the fact that we continually and constantly talk to ourselves. We also went over the extreme power of the brain and visualization. Now, for a brief moment, we are going to control the conversation and picture in our minds. We are going to do this with what psychologists refer to as mental contrasting and implementation. This strategy has been proven to increase performance in academic outcomes and adherence to physical training programs. Note: studies show the results have lasting effects for about 16 weeks. So as Zig Ziglar said, "People often say that motivation doesn't last. Well, neither does bathing—that's why we recommend it daily." This is an internal communication strategy you will want to repeat every few months.

INTERNAL COMMUNICATION

The process is simple. After you have your goal set in the "Navigate" phase, visualize and ask yourself, "If I accomplish this goal, what is the best attainable result?" Imagine the best possible outcome. Next, look for the obstacle, visualize and then ask yourself, "What might prevent me from accomplishing this goal?". Look, you aren't perfect, and even superman has kryptonite, so visualize, and then think realistically about what, in your daily life, could stop you from accomplishing your goal. Finally, make your plan for this nuisance. Visualize and ask yourself, "What's an effective way to tackle this obstacle?"

Walk through that process and spend time visualizing and asking yourself these questions and coming up with good answers. Next, we start communicating with others.

EXTERNAL COMMUNICATION

A study conducted by Gail Matthews found that people with written goals are 39% more likely to achieve them. All you need to do is write down your goal to increase your likelihood of achieving it. What's even cooler is that the same study found if you send your progress to friends or family for accountability, your likelihood of achieving your goal jumps to 76.7%.

The fact is, this book exists because every other month I meet with a group of high-level entrepreneurs to whom I am accountable for doing what I say. After slow-rolling chapter by chapter, I finally told the group I was going to finish this book, and then I told them exactly when I would finish it. Generally, there's no punishment for not doing what you say you will do. Still, based on some elementary psychology, we all want to maintain consistent behavior and make sure our actions align with our statements.

I've walked thousands through a similar process, and now you get to do it too. First, get 20 blank index cards or sheets of paper. Second, make a list of the 10 people you care about most. Write your goal on all 20 cards or sheets of paper and make sure it says what you are going to do and the date by when you are going to do it. Next, mail or hand out 10 of the cards/paper to the people you care about most. Finally, hand out the remaining cards/paper to people who are not on your top 10 list. These could be neighbors, co-workers, colleagues, etc., people you interact with on a fairly regular basis.

The last part of this equation requires that you check in with someone regularly about progress you've made towards your goal. I've found friends and family can be too forgiving at times, so join a group, hire a coach, or utilize anyone who you know won't take your excuses and who will tell you like it is.

So what happens after you achieve your goal or when you don't struggle to get things done?

GIVING ADVICE

Remember, your relationships and social interactions are some of the most significant determining factors in your longevity, so no matter your ability to stick to a plan/achieve a goal, if you're a hermit, it won't be a worthwhile pursuit.

The final phase of external communication concerns the giving of advice. It's important to do and I offer two explanations for why I think so: scientific and relational.

Let's start with science. A 2018 study conducted by The Wharton School at the University of Pennsylvania involving over 2,000 participants, revealed the power of giving advice. They found individuals were more motivated by giving advice than receiving it, even if they were currently struggling with achieving their goals.

Interestingly, across domains, people predicted the opposite, expecting themselves and others to be less motivated by giving advice than receiving it. This phenomenon replicated across self-regulatory fields: strugglers who offered advice, compared to those who received expert advice, were more motivated to save money, control their tempers, lose weight, and seek employment.

Giving unsolicited advice to your friends and family doesn't build the best relationships but, if and when you can, do it anyway. There are hundreds of ways you can communicate advice in conversation and to like-minded groups. You could even start a blog or podcast and kickstart the process, but remember—don't be a hermit.

And now, the human/relational reason for giving advice. Confucius claimed that, "He who governs by means of his virtue is like the pole-star: it remains in its place while all the lesser stars do homage to it."

If you genuinely are achieving mastery in any field or endeavor, I believe it is on you to communicate that information as widely as you can. When you talk about what you've achieved, you become better because in order to explain something correctly, you must refine and simplify your method. Also, you help others around you step up their game and become a better version of themselves.

No one succeeds alone.

TAKEAWAYS

1. **Always Sound Cool.** Avoid the three communication mistakes: Communicating Too Early, Communicating in Fragments, and Communicating Excitement.
2. **Never Communicate Too Early.** People should know you are serious before you begin something new.
3. **No One Succeeds Alone.** Don't force your way through. Embrace those around you.

PART 3: RESULTS

THE 86% PROCESS

86%

The intentional pursuit of purposeful discomfort can act as a compass telling you where you need to go, but it does not prepare you for the journey.

However, there is a tempo we can tap into which casts ease aside, and dives into the delicate simplicity of Killing Comfort: **The 86% Process**

The wolf fails 86% of the time, yet still wins. But, that 86% hurts. It is continual effort with marginal progress. However, it's a combination of these daily and weekly actions repeated over and over that sharpen the skills which provide for the 14% success.

For us, we must hone in on our daily habits, push ourselves to a level we are ready for, get laser-focused on what we want, and avoid the mistakes that will hold us back. These things work together in a subtle symphony, like pistons in an engine, each must fire in the right order to keep us moving forward. Firing on only one, or two, prevents the formation of the essential links that are required to create extraordinary results. Understanding this synergistic relationship is at the core of unlocking the prerequisite for astounding success.

If I haven't made it abundantly clear, the 86% process I lay out over the next several chapters is not easy. It will take mental fortitude, it will take grit—something that seems to be vanishing.

DISAPPEARING GRIT

Grit is disappearing, and it's an epidemic.

Your great grandparents practiced grit daily; it was called living a hard life. Now, we have too many conveniences and easy buttons. Our brains are becoming mush— motivation is nonexistent and pushing ourselves is rare.

The fact is, you can build up your mental toughness, your grit, your will power, your brainpower, your focus, and your cognitive function by taking small steps every day.

I am sure you have some questions, just like I did. Questions such as:

- Why do some people seem to have endless internal motivation while others are drained at the end of every day?
- Why do some have rock-solid performance in life and the gym, while others plateau?
- And why are some people dangerously effective while others flounder?

Over the next few chapters of this book, I'll share the answers to these questions so you, too, can become a dangerously effective human.

Following the aviate - navigate - communicate process is essential to seeing results. Still, the levers you pull there are high-level, so now we are going to dive into the tactical approaches to discomfort and extraordinary results.

I've learned that motivation is not a mythical unicorn that can't be captured. While discipline will always trump motivation, motivation can be better harnessed through your lifestyle.

If you're a person who lacks discipline and you aren't getting results, or you're an experienced and disciplined person who isn't leveraging this remarkable ability to see the results, you should stay with me. You're going to discover how people like you and me can increase our motivation and perform better and why it's critical you get these basics handled right now.

The goal of Part 3 of this book is simple: To help you become a dangerously effective human by following the 86% process.

First, your mental toughness score will be revealed in our Mental Toughness Audit. Without a good gauge here, you can't understand what challenges will best fit you. Then, I'll make a case for meeting yourself, pushing yourself to the point where your internal chatter is counteracting your desire. Now, I get this "meet yourself" approach may be different from what you've heard before. But this fundamental shift is one reason why this process is so effective.

We will also hit on the elements needed for success in any arena and the fitness that supports better performance and longevity.

I've been developing and refining our framework for close to a decade. I've been trying to help people like you with the mental side of the game for years. I want you to start and stick to the things you desire and see massive results. But there's always a challenge in the mind game.

For a long time, I would tell people to be more disciplined, but that didn't work. Don't get me wrong...discipline truly does equal freedom. However, I knew there had to be something elemental to motivation and discipline—a trainable trait.

We've worked with thousands of people over the last ten years and our results speak for themselves. The results framework I am about to present is simple, but it is not easy. I know once I got past what I *thought* I knew, I started seeing massive results. I began to embrace focus and simplicity and extraordinary results ensued.

And if you're ready to become dangerously effective, let's get right to it.

13. BALANCE

"That which does not kill us makes us stronger." Friedrich Nietzsche

Working hard for your family is good. Too much hard work can lead to burnout, depression, and poor health.

It's as if nature intended all facets of our existence to exist in delicate balance. It's our job to counterbalance our life's stressors. Failure to do so will lead to physical or mental breakdown.

Your body is always in a battle to maintain homeostasis. Anything that disrupts your body's craving for homeostasis causes stress—not the type of stress you get from work—but stress on your biological system. When you disrupt your body's quest for homeostasis, it fights back.

The good news is, every time you drag your body through this process of homeostasis disruption, your body then super-compensates or adapts, according to the general adaptation principle. This is what creates fantastic results from exercise. But if all you do is breakdown and never build up, you're going to have some trouble. Let's explore how to maintain balance in this psychological and physiological stress-inducing world.

BALANCE THROUGH ELEMENTS

Several years ago, I started tracking everything: exercise volume, water intake, macronutrients, micronutrients, sets, reps, heart rate variability, resting heart rate, sleep, and the list goes on.

I quickly concluded that tracking everything helped nothing. Tracking is simply awareness. Knowing your resting heart rate gives you some insight into your fitness level, but not much. If you cannot manipulate or change anything you are tracking, then, what's the point?

Tracking personal health and fitness data that cannot be manipulated is at best interesting trivia, and at worst a complete waste of your time. However, personal health and fitness data that can be manipulated is a massive performance advantage in every aspect of your life.

Once I realized how to manipulate my health and fitness data, I started to see massive performance-metric improvements. Initially, the experiment for all this was an $n = 1$ situation, i.e., just me. Now, we have thousands of athletes self-reporting, and we have millions of data points.

We have cross-referenced this data with years worth of information on resting heart rate (RHR), sleep, etc., together with some subjective measures.

Every single week, we ask each athlete who works with us some simple questions. The most exciting thing we've found is that the athletes who are seeing the most results have the highest adherence to "the game."

Over time, we gradually changed "game" to what we now call the "EO3 Elements." The EO3 Elements are habits we consider to be essential to success. We found that not only did our game help athletes recover, but this set of habits built a better human, in the gym or at work, by creating a way to balance and combat the stress of daily life. These are not athletic habits reserved for athletes, rather they're basic guidelines that help people live a better life. The elements we teach will accelerate your results in every area.

BIG IDEA: EO3 ELEMENTS

As you know, one small action can lead to a series of self-sustaining reactions that we call chain reactions. Chain reactions can produce a lot of momentum, power, and energy.

The energy created by a simple chain reaction can be explosive.

In 1983, Lorne Whitehead wrote in the American Journal of Physics that a falling domino could do much more than knock down another domino of equal size. The force from one falling domino can topple a second domino 1.5 times its size.

To put this in perspective, imagine starting a chain reaction by pushing a two-inch domino into another one that is 1.5 times larger, successively. By the time the 17th domino falls, it is able to knock down a domino close to the size of the Leaning Tower of

Pisa. Furthermore, domino 23 would be taller than
the Eiffel Tower, domino 31 would be 3,000 feet taller
than Mount Everest, and domino 57 would be almost
equal to the distance from the earth to the moon!

Committing to the EO3 Elements is something that
should be done daily over decades; think of it as a
leading domino. To start, we recommend treating it
as a game where you get one point for every item you
complete. Rather than aiming for perfection, aim for
as many points as you can each day. Over time, this
game will transform into a habit. Once these habits
become a part of who you are, your life will
dramatically change. You will forever be primed for
high performance mentally and physically. This is
the foundation we build better humans on. Commit
today and develop the habits. Dialing in your lifestyle
parameters is the BIGGEST first step you can take to
improve mental acuity, balance energy levels, and
increase performance.

Any stressor, including athletic training, can be bad
for you. So yes, physical exercise can be bad for you
if it is not countered with proper recovery.

Don't believe me? Try hitting a hard training cycle
while working 80 hours a week. Grossly under eat,
avoid micronutrients, drink very little water, sleep as
little as you can, drink three beers each night, and
never see the sun, then see what happens.

Now, the good (and kind of bad) thing is that your
body is an AMAZING adaptation machine. Sure, you
can continue to do things the way you've always done
them and your body will continue adapting to the
minimum standards you provide it, until, eventually,
it won't. This is when you become sick, broken, or

dead. Or, less dramatically, you'll never see the result you want, you'll never reach your potential, and you will never discover your true capabilities. It would be easy to just blame your lack of achievement on genetics, right?

PLAYING THE GAME: THE ELEMENTS

The purpose of the elements is to help you build habits that improve performance, enhance results, and make you a better human!

The purpose of the game is not to add stress to your life or to become an obsession.

With that in mind, here are our elements:

1. **SLEEP:** Did you get 7+ hours of sleep last night?

2. **HYDRATION + MINERAL BALANCE:** Did you consume 50-60% of your bodyweight (lb) in ounces of water today?

3. **NUTRITION:** Did you eat protein + veggies in two meals today?

4. **WARM-UP/COOL-DOWN:** Did you complete a 5-min warmup and cooldown during your exercise?

5. **MEAL TIMING:** Has your body fasted for at least 12 hours?

6. **DIGESTION:** Chew food. Smell food. Limit liquids during eating.

7. **BLOOD FLOW:** Light aerobic work (walk, jog) for 10 min outside of regular training?

8. **ADEQUATE SUN EXPOSURE:** Vitamin D

9. **DOWN-REGULATION:** Meditation. Breathing. Limit Nighttime Light Exposure.

The only goal is to gain as many points as you can each day and not to be perfect.

You could have a stressful day at work or home, get a sunburn, or one of a hundred other things that can prevent your body from achieving balance.

It is your body's adaptation to a stressor that gives you results in physical fitness. How well you adapt to that stressor is, in part, how well you can recover or provide the raw materials needed for adaptation and recovery.

Each of these nine areas could be a book in and of itself, so I will not expound greatly on any one. Do know that it took me and my team years of research and thousands of athlete data points to finally decide these nine were of most importance. I encourage you to use this as a launchpad for your own research.

1. Sleep is your superpower and it seems to have a hand in almost every biological process we have. Pay it the respect it deserves.

2. Hydration goes beyond consuming liquid. Be sure you get the proper minerals on a daily basis, too. Dehydration can affect hunger cravings and cause mental fog. We challenge

our athletes to consume 50% of their body weight, in ounces of water, each day.

3. Your chosen lifestyle and exercise type greatly determine how much protein you need. Don't neglect the only building block your body has. Combine high-quality protein with vegetables for superior health. The goal is to reduce/avoid creating inflammation as much as possible.

4. Warming up and cooling down greatly decrease your chance of injury during exercise—don't skip either.

5. Going twelve hours without eating is pretty common for some and for others not at all. Eating without breaks sends your insulin levels on a continuous rollercoaster ride. Try to give your digestive system a break for at least 12 hours each day.

6. Speaking of digestion, quit swallowing your food whole. There is a mechanical process involved in digestion, and it is called chewing. Chew your food well to make sure your body can extract all the nutrients.

7. Additional aerobic work can be as simple as walking the dog or playing outside with your kids. Blood flow brings nutrients to and from parts of your body. Try to move regularly to make this as easy as possible on your biological system.

8. Humans are powered by the sun. Get enough sun exposure for your skin type to provide a

sufficient amount of Vitamin D. Vitamin D has been shown to decrease illness and injury rates as well as improve strength and endurance. There's also the bonus element of simply being outside, getting fresh air, and letting natural sunlight set your circadian rhythm.

9. Having some sort of down-regulation process at night will help lower cortisol, improve your sleep, and give you a better sense of well-being. Try limiting blue light by wearing blue-light-blocking glasses, read a book instead of watching TV, and start a breathing practice or meditation.

Hormesis is a way to stress the body positively, but it is stress nonetheless. That is why daily practice of the elements is paramount.

TAKEAWAYS

1. **Elements.** The elements are the prerequisite to being a high-performer. Don't skip them. Practice daily.
2. **Not Perfection.** Try to get in as many elements each day. Even a few will help tremendously. Do not worry if you cannot get all nine into every day.
3. **Break, then Build.** Every stressor needs to be counterbalanced. Keep that in mind when you pursue hard things.

14. FOCUS

"Nothing in this world can take the place of persistence. Talent will not; nothing is more common than unsuccessful people with talent. Genius will not; unrewarded genius is almost a proverb. Education will not; the world is full of educated derelicts. Persistence and determination alone are omnipotent. The slogan "press on" has solved and always will solve the problems of the human race"
Calvin Coolidge

There once was a successful accountant who hated his 9 to 5 cubicle existence.

It took him 23 years to, as he put it, "...awaken from what I consider a long slow nightmare." Finally, fed up enough, he sold all of his possessions, bought a sailboat, and has been sailing around the world with his wife ever since.

14. FOCUS

He didn't know what he was going to do next after he quit his job, but he did set a litmus test for making a decision: "...this next thing you do must be so interesting to you that you will stay up all night learning about it." Chasing a childhood dream, he turned to sailing. It passed his test.

Do you have any such rules or tests for your life?

I want to urge you to strip away the non-essential, and pursue one thing as opposed to scattering your efforts and getting scattered results. I urged you earlier in this book, to take a shot at articulating what your purpose is. Now, we are going to dive a little bit deeper. While I cannot reveal to you your purpose, I would like to lead you as far along the path as possible to finding your one thing, your purpose, or what you live for.

I know, it sounds a bit heavy. Are you uncomfortable yet? If you are uncomfortable at the idea of unearthing your purpose, it's for one of two reasons. Reason #1, it's a big freaking deal and you don't want to screw it up. Reason #2, you have some string that is too short to be saved, i.e., an idea holding you back that is causing you to denigrate the very idea of finding a purpose. If you are uncomfortable, that's good.

I find the concept of discovering your "one thing" to be challenging for people to wrap their minds around. So tricky, in fact, I frequently see people give up out of frustration.

Having one thing is a mission statement for your life. It's a litmus test for decisions. It helps you focus so that you can pursue extraordinary results.

Setting a principle or idea as a guiding light for your life, for your business, and your family is a powerful thing.

Once you have this one thing, decisions get easier, and you are less likely to pursue the next shiny object by jumping from one thing to the next.

To gain a better understanding of the one-thing concept, let's take a look at some of the most well known business titans in American history: John D. Rockefeller, Thomas A. Edison, and Henry Ford.

Observe how they each had one thing. They did not chase shiny objects. Perhaps the most powerful attribute of their focus is that when each of their missions was combined with each others' it led to unfathomable results instead of narrow marginal results.

ROCKEFELLER'S ONE THING

John D. Rockefeller once wrote to one of his partners, "Let the good work go on. We must ever remember we are refining oil for the poor man, and he must have it cheap and good."

In the early days of oil, Rockefeller built his fortune by illuminating the homes of America guided by this principle, his one thing: making oil cheap and also good. Before electricity, Rockefeller delivered kerosene to homes all around the country and lit the lamps of a nation and beyond.

While Rockefeller eventually secured a monopoly on oil, it was not because he lacked competitors. Rockefeller did not focus solely on discovering crude oil. Instead, he focused heavily on the refinement of that oil to keep the price down and to deliver a product that was of the highest quality.

His competitors did not share this goal. Many of his competitors rushed the refinement process and delivered dangerous kerosene that was too volatile, igniting fires and burning down houses. When the public is given the choice of safe vs. unsafe, a business gets a lot easier to run.

His one thing of "cheap and good" led Rockefeller to be the best at the refinement of crude oil, which would continue to serve him later in business.

EDISON ARRIVES

Rockefeller had an excellent run illuminating homes all around the world with cheap and good kerosene for lamps, but then Edison arrived onto the scene. The story of the light bulb began long before Edison patented the first commercially successful bulb in 1879. Still, he was the first to be able to turn the electric light bulb into an industry that would extinguish the flames of kerosene lamps.

Edison's one thing was very similar to Rockefeller's. Edison did not merely want to make the best light bulb, nor did he rush to create something that could be unsafe. Where Edison succeeded and surpassed his competition was in developing a practical and inexpensive light bulb. Similar to Rockefeller, Edison was focusing on making something of high quality that would have practical use on a large scale.

At this point, Rockefeller was no slouch, and his Standard Oil Company controlled 95% of U.S. oil refineries. He could have easily bought Edison out, shut him down, or at the very least, become a significant investor with controlling interest. The fact that Edison had to take on investors like J.P. Morgan is proof enough that he needed capital to pursue his one thing.

For Edison to light up the homes of America with an incandescent light bulb, he had to focus on the creation of power plants. To make his one thing come to life, he had to focus on something besides the light bulb: the distribution of electricity to power that light bulb.

Just like Rockefeller was not focused on the lamp, but was instead focused on the oil refinement process, Edison had to focus less on the device and instead turn instead to the distribution of electricity.

Rockefeller did not see the next big thing, get excited, and change his principles. He did not scatter his resources to pursue electricity.

Even though Edison's one thing did stand to disrupt and dismantle Rockefeller's business completely, Rockefeller didn't waiver and also wrote to one of his partners, "I hope we can continue to hold out with the best illuminator in the world at the lowest price."

And it was Rockefeller's resolve and commitment to his one thing that proved to be most important.

FORD CHANGES THE GAME

In August of 1899, as Edison was fighting the battle of alternating current vs. direct current (that he eventually lost to Nikola Tesla) Henry Ford resigned as chief engineer at the Edison Illuminating Company, in Detroit, Michigan, to concentrate on automobile production.

Similar to Edison and the lightbulb, Ford was not the first person to invent the automobile. Many automobiles were already in existence before Henry Ford appeared on the scene. However, Ford's one thing was to deliver affordable, high-quality machines to the working man.

Ford's creation of the assembly line exploded the production of automobiles. Automobiles which needed gas to run.

Luckily for Rockefeller, a by-product created by his kerosene refinement process, was a highly volatile substance that had been discarded as waste. This discard would come to be known as gasoline and it was the perfect fuel not only for Ford's automobiles but also for his plants that were illuminated by incandescent light bulbs and fueled by oil.

Each man had a relentless commitment to one thing. And it was not simply each man's one thing that made him the titan we know today. It is the intersection of Ford's and Edison's one thing that made the world what it is today. Both of considerable means, either could have chased new ideas, pursued different interests, and would have had some success. However, the fact that neither man wavered from his one thing proved to be paramount.

Rockefeller would not have been as successful without Ford's automobiles and the innovation of the assembly line.

Edison would not have seen his dreams come to life if it wasn't for Nikola Tesla's dedication to humankind and the development of alternating electrical current.

We can glean three big lessons from these giants.

First, each titan had a prominent one thing that drove him forward. All had a mission to pursue and a guiding light to keep them on track. When a new opportunity arose, all that each man had to do was ask himself if it fit his mission. If the answer was no, he wouldn't pursue the new venture.

Second, in order to pursue this one thing, each man often had to consider alternative strategies. They were quick to adapt and quick to recognize futile strategies. Each man surveyed his environment and recognized how his one thing would have to adapt to change, and then he would execute.

Third, none of them succeeded alone. Each man became the best at what he did and used his one thing, sometimes leveraging another man's one thing, to catapult himself to extraordinary achievement.

TAKEAWAYS

1. **Success = Focus.** You don't become wildly successful by becoming a jack of all trades. If you want success, you must be a master of one.
2. **Don't Chase Shiny Objects.** Every time you get excited about something new and change course, you lose. It can't be measured, but the cost of not staying the course can be insurmountable.
3. **Be Steadfast.** Don't second guess yourself once you have made a decision. Instead, look for alternatives when you face a challenge.

15. GRIT

"The impediment to action advances action. What stands in the way becomes the way." **Marcus Aurelius**

After leaving the military, I started down the path of athletic coaching with a militant mindset. I had checklists and procedures for everything. The assessments I developed left no room for guesswork and helped me to dial things in for each athlete.

I wanted athletes to achieve all of the success they desired. It didn't matter what the goal was, I was extremely confident that if they followed my plan, they would see success.

I learned quickly that every single person I worked with was unique. Aside from the differences in physiology and goals, there existed a considerable gap, psychologically. Some athletes would do everything I suggested, some would do one or two things, and some athletes would do nothing.

I had a hard time wrapping my brain around the fact that some people would pay for a service and not use

147

it. Furthermore, why did others stick to the plan and see results without struggling at all?

The idea that some people "do" and some people "don't," an idea I got from a lot of other coaches, was not an OK answer for me. I wasn't going to let people come to me for help and then walk away in the same condition in which they arrived.

Then it hit me. I was assessing the wrong things. Every coach I know does some sort of assessment. I was performing a very basic assessment to create a movement-based program and provide nutrition advice.

I realized my assessment was rudimentary and didn't set anyone up for success. It would be similar to buying a new car after only checking the oil, the tires, the interior, and exterior for imperfections, and then immediately signing the paperwork to buy the car.

There's just one issue. How much can you know about the car if you never turn it on and drive it around? That's what I needed to do with new athletes. Without becoming a licensed psychologist, I needed to find out what was going on between the ears first, and how they handled life, before I could even think about assessing them physically or talking about nutrition.

I began to study and conduct extensive research on elite performers, self-determination theory, goal-setting, and mental toughness. My goal was to come up with a pre-assessment, one that would assess someone's sticking power, before I could get into assessing fitness and nutrition.

Over time, and with one athlete at a time, I tested new ideas and strategies to boost sticking power and to find out how to best work with athletes who seemed high or low on the motivation, mental toughness, and sticking power scales. It took a long time to find what worked and what didn't work.

But, after each version and refinement, I came up with what we now call the "Mental Toughness Audit." A series of a few simple questions I ask new athletes to assess their mental toughness potential.

Based on a straightforward audit of someone's mental toughness, I can hone in on how to coach them. The Mental Toughness Audit is not a predictor of success or failure. Instead, it reveals how much an athlete can realistically take on and still succeed.

After implementing the Mental Toughness Audit with athletes, stick rates climbed dramatically. This new approach changed the game for me and the other coaches. It helped us lead athletes who never thought they could, or who had failed in the past, to extraordinary results.

Now, I'd like to walk you through our mental toughness audit. By answering the questions, you will learn a little bit more about yourself, about what you should put on your plate and how you should tackle your goals.

ASSESS GRIT: THE AUDIT

The simplicity of the audit is what makes it practical to use. These questions were not pulled out of thin air. Instead, they were developed by looking at the research on elite performers conducted by the

15. GRIT

Cardiff School of Sport in addition to papers published on Self-Determination Theory.

Here are the six questions included in our Mental Toughness Audit along with notes on how to score each item. You can assess yourself or someone else. Each question requires an open-ended response. There are no right or wrong answers. Each item is scored, using a point system, based on the response given. Let's begin:

1. *What is your goal?*	Score
Extrinsic goal: an outward or worldly goal such as lose weight, make money, build muscle, win award, e.g.,	0
Intrinsic goal: an inward goal relating to oneself, such as improve relationships, good health, reduce stress, etc.	1

2. *Do you have a mentor(s) or peers that you look toward for guidance?*	Score
No mentors/peer group.	0
One or more mentors/peer group.	1
Note: One essential trait of successful human beings is to team up with a peer group or a mentor.	

3. *What is the biggest challenge you have overcome?*	Score
No significant challenges.	0
At least one significant challenge.	1
Note: Most people will respond positively to this question. Challenges can be of any type, physical, life, emotional, etc.	

4. *If you felt like skipping out on a daily commitment, what would you do?*	Score
No strategy.	0
Uses self-talk or other psychological strategy to overcome tough stuff, cravings, skipping workouts, etc.	1

5. *A lot of people want to achieve (insert goal from question 1 here). What makes your desire greater than those who will fail to attain this goal?*	Score
Little to no desire to succeed.	0
Insatiable desire to succeed.	1
Note: Scoring this question will be somewhat subjective. Ask yourself, how badly do they want it?	

6. *How supportive are your family and friends of your goal?*	Score
Little to no support.	0
Has support.	1
Note: Dig deep here. Most people will say they have support but do they really? Do friends and family support the habits, schedule, lifestyle required to attain the goal?	

Mental Toughness Audit	Total Score
These individuals will struggle to stick to things and will succeed more often when working on one task at a time. I.e., Work on consistency before introducing any other changes. The need for intervention and accountability will be paramount for these individuals.	0 to 3
These individuals will succeed at a high level, often able to juggle multiple tasks. Provide these individuals with robust rules and principles to guide them on any endeavor.	4 to 6
Note: The Mental Toughness Audit only assesses potential. An individual who has a high score but hasn't practiced mental toughness, has all of the raw materials to succeed, yet might struggle to achieve genuine success. Individuals with low scores can increase their potential over time, scoring higher in subsequent audits.	

15. GRIT

Your turn.

Q1: What is your goal?

_____

_____

_____

_____

Q2: Do you have any mentors or peers you look up to right now?

_____

_____

_____

_____

Q3: What is the biggest challenge you have overcome?

_____

_____

_____

_____

15. GRIT

Q4: If you felt like skipping out on a daily commitment, what would you do?

_____

_____

_____

_____

Q5: A lot of people want to achieve (insert goal from Q1). What makes your desire greater than those who fail?

_____

_____

_____

_____

Q6: How supportive are your friends/family of your goal?

_____

_____

_____

_____

A reminder here—the Mental Toughness Audit only assesses potential. An individual who has a high score but has not practiced mental toughness, has all of the raw materials to succeed, yet might struggle to achieve genuine success. Individuals with low scores can increase potential over time, scoring higher in subsequent audits.

The audit puts you on the same playing field with the individual you are assessing. Some people have experienced hardship that you and I cannot imagine and would never know about if we hadn't asked. While others have the appearance of toughness but have never dealt with anything more challenging than a late Amazon delivery. The audit removes assumptions and gives you a starting framework.

So how do we continue to build grit based on the different scores? The audit simply lets you know where you may want to start. Here are some suggestions:

BUILD GRIT: STRIPPING THE NONESSENTIAL (SCORE 0-3)

So what happens if you have a low score? First, know that even elite performers struggle. And no matter the caliber of the person I am working with, when struggle appears, my process is the same.

Strip away the nonessential. This is suggested mainly for those who score 3 or less but is good practice for everyone.

15. GRIT

Behavioral modification is the only direction to go if the basics of just getting started are challenging. If you can't stick to working out five days per week, four days per week, or even two days per week, then, let's focus on one day per week for 10 minutes.

This action, though, will not be what is needed for significant physiological change to occur. However, it will be the catalyst in the psychological transformation that will compound, producing more significant results in the future.

When people are struggling with the basics, I coach them using a process I developed called the 17-second process.

If you have a hard time forming a habit or sticking to things, then I only need you to do one thing. Focus on what you want your life to be like for 17 seconds, once a day. For 17 seconds, close your eyes and visualize what you want to achieve. Do this every day for 100 days. Do not miss a day. To some, this suggestion will seem hilarious or offensively easy. Remember the Reticular Activating System from Chapter 8? We are going to put it to work while building up your basic "stick to it" skill.

Speaking of things I've thought were hilarious and offensively easy...

On my first day of pilot training, I was issued a poster, rolled up, with a rubber band around it. When I unrolled the poster, I realized it was a replica image of the cockpit of the aircraft we were flying. I jokingly asked one of the instructor pilots if I was supposed to decorate my house with this poster to which he responded, "It's for chair flying."

In short, chair flying is putting a plunger between your legs, stating radio calls to no one, and pressing pretend buttons on a piece of paper. When I first heard of chair flying, I laughed. It sounded ridiculously easy because the challenge of flying is rarely in the button-pressing or radio calls and more in the unknown events that can transpire during any given sortie.

I was incredulous (and arrogant) because I knew that there were state of the art flight simulators, aircraft that could fly faster than the speed of sound, and world-class instructors at every turn, but our first step was to play pilot with a poster on the wall?

I wasn't ready for the simulators, mach speed, or world-class instruction. I needed to memorize and never miss calls. I needed to practice simple actions, day after day, until they were burned into my memory. I needed to develop the habit of action.

The 17-second process is the habit of action we're looking to build over those 100 days that I just mentioned. Every time you mess up, the clock gets reset, and you go back to zero.

If you are the type of person who cannot stick to things for more than a few days or weeks, the 17-second process is where you begin. Drop the ego and become a person who can start and stick to things.

BUILD GRIT: MEET YOURSELF SATURDAY (SCORE 4-6)

So what happens if you have a high score? Scoring slightly higher on the audit simply means you may be able to stick to things more quickly than others. If you are equipped with this superpower, then the question becomes how do we continue to build your grit?

The answer: Meet yourself regularly.

In stoic philosophy, the practice of voluntary discomfort is common. Seneca, a Roman Stoic philosopher, said;

> Set aside a certain number of days, during which you shall be content with the scantiest and cheapest fare, with coarse and rough dress, saying to yourself the while: "Is this the condition that I feared?" It is precisely in times of immunity from care that the soul should toughen itself beforehand for occasions of greater stress, and it is while Fortune is kind that it should fortify itself against her violence. In days of peace the soldier performs maneuvers, throws up earthworks with no enemy in sight, and wearies himself by gratuitous toil, in order that he may be equal to unavoidable toil. If you would not have a man flinch when the crisis comes, train him before it comes.

Putting oneself in uncomfortable situations to gain a better perspective was practiced in many different ways among stoics. Some would wear shabby clothes, some would brave the elements while inadequately dressed, others would simply forgo the pleasure of saying yes to something desirable.

In my world, I don't know of any better way to do what Seneca is talking about than to attempt difficult physical challenges, regularly.

In fitness, benchmarking your performance is easy. If you run a 7-minute mile today, and then you run a 6-minute mile 12 months later, that is a significant improvement of your benchmark. However, how do we set mental benchmarks?

The idea of mental benchmarking is simple...find out when you quit, or when you most want to quit, and write it down. The goal is to extend this benchmark as much as you can over time.

Push yourself until you find that voice inside of your head who wants to quit, who wants to slow down, and who doesn't want to push it as hard. When you hear that voice, note when it happened, at what point in the workout, and why it happened. Now, you have a mental benchmark.

I started mental benchmarking when I dedicated myself to doing the workout "MURPH" every week for a year. If you are not familiar with the workout, here it is.

MURPH

For time:

- 1 mile Run
- 100 Pull-ups
- 200 Push-ups
- 300 Squats
- 1 mile Run

Partition the pull-ups, push-ups, and squats as needed. Start and finish with a 1-mile run. If you've got a twenty-pound vest or body armor, wear it.

This workout was created in the memory of Navy Lieutenant Michael Murphy, 29, of Patchogue, N.Y., who was killed in Afghanistan on June 28th, 2005.

Each time I would do MURPH, there would be a moment in the workout where the voice in my head would start to bargain to get me to slow down, or even stop. I would note where and when it happened and keep moving.

Over time, I started to call this "meeting yourself." When all the niceties and layers of comfort have been stripped away, you get to have a conversation with who you are. You can shape and mold this deep version of yourself, but only when you push hard enough to find it.

Each time I didn't listen to that voice in my head, I found it harder and harder to find that voice the next time. Now, having completed the workout hundreds of times, I can't find that voice. My mental benchmark has been pushed so far, it takes more significant duration and exertion to "meet myself," and that's the point.

One thing I learned by doing infrequent and occasional challenges was that meeting yourself once or twice a year is not enough. It's a practice that needs to be cultivated regularly to see genuine progress.

What started as simple internal dialog has turned into a mental toughness revolution. In our community, we have thousands of athletes who participate in what we call "Meet Yourself Saturday" workouts every week.

Meet yourself Saturday is pretty simple. We do really hard workouts on Saturday. The kind of workouts that require you to "meet yourself" i.e., when you start to question if you should quit, slow down, or tap out. This training will improve your mental fitness just as much as your physical fitness.

A majority of the time, I prefer to lean on science and intelligence when pursuing fitness. On Saturday, we throw the playbook out the window. While safety and knowing your physical limitations when implementing a Meet Yourself Saturday workout is of the utmost importance, sometimes, to pursue grit, you have to get uncomfortable. Meet Yourself Saturday is not an excuse for pushing yourself to injury, nor is it the place for stupidity. Safely pushing yourself under the supervision of a coach is possible.

Regularly pushing yourself and doing hard things will translate to your job, your family life, and your fitness. Stick with it for a couple of months, and you will be surprised about who you become.

YOUR BRICK WALL

After the 100 days of the 17-Seconds process, mental benchmarking, Meet Yourself Saturdays are the next step. The next logical question that often arises is, how often do I need to "meet myself"?

In a 2009 study published in the European Journal of Social Psychology, Phillippa Lally and her research team decided to figure out just how long it takes to form a habit.

Phillippa et al., determined that it took 18 to 254 days for a behavior to become a habit. Many have referred to this study when attempting to debunk the "21-days to a new habit" idea that has been perpetuated for years. If you dig deeper into the study, you'll find the magic number of days to form a new habit to be 66 days, but I think anything worth doing is worth overdoing. So, I suggest going to the outside limits of the research so we won't miss it. Furthermore, since meeting yourself isn't something you should do daily, let's settle on 254...workouts that is, but let's call them bricks.

Something I encourage all of our athletes to do is to create a physical representation of the bricks when you do these tough workouts so that you can prevail in spite of the negative self-talk.

In the past, I have used actual bricks and refer to it as building my brick wall. At the end of the year, after numerous tough physical challenges, it is very satisfying to see a wall of bricks representing the things you have overcome. You can use lego bricks, stones, and if you have real bricks, those work, too.

15. GRIT

Building your mental toughness is like building a house... you have to start with the foundation, then you can begin laying brick or stone. You have to fortify your mind, condition it to be tough, and then build a wall between you and mental weakness.

Each brick will be a workout session during which you get comfortable in the uncomfortable. While you're working out, imagine that you are building your wall of mental toughness. I'm talking about 254 legitimate mental toughness training sessions. If you make it to this number, there won't be much that can be thrown at you, that you can't handle.

First, let's get clear about the definition of a brick. A brick represents any time you find yourself in an uncomfortable position, but you cope and get comfortable in the uncomfortable. Maybe it is a smile you muster amid the pain and discomfort you feel when doing burpees as fast as possible. Or, perhaps it's keeping a level head when your heart and respiratory rates are jacked.

To develop mental toughness, you will need the willpower and discipline to get out of your comfort zone. This is not what average people do. Live by this principle and you will accomplish something much more significant than plain average. Every time you decide to push yourself, you set a brick. Each brick builds upon the last brick. Your mental toughness is increasing, and so are the results you see.

Now, don't be thrown off by the "comfortable in the uncomfortable" phrase. You may never actually find a sense of pure enjoyment in pushing your body hard, but you CAN get comfortable when you decide to put yourself in that position and to stay there. You may be afraid, but if you face your fear one time, you become courageous. Do it again, and you gain more courage. Instead of a brick wall, you have an impenetrable brick house.

The amygdala is going to recognize, as a primal instinct (that you have no control over), what you are doing in these training sessions as fear. The next stop for this fear is the cortex or frontal lobe. This is where your brain has an opportunity to concentrate, reason, and bring structure to the chaos. This is your opportunity to flood the amygdala with positive self-talk that is based on the premise of visualization. Likewise, visualizing the exercise before it takes place helps greatly in being comfortable in the uncomfortable.

Be in control of your mind, do not let it control you, and you are there! This is how you build your brick wall—one victory at a time.

Let's get back to building that wall, every time you feel you have earned a brick, take your Lego, stone, or brick and write the date you earned it. If you use Lego bricks, build it on a Lego base. If you use stones, write the date on the stones and put them into a mason jar.

Your goal is 254 bricks.

If you are in our community and participate in one of these sessions each Saturday, that's one brick. This means it will take you nearly five years to build a brick wall of 254 bricks, and that's OK. No one said this would be quick or easy.

TAKEAWAYS

1. **Assess.** You can't know where you are going until you know where you are.
2. **Go Small.** If you fail to stick to something, go smaller and smaller until you can get it done.
3. **Meet Yourself.** Find a version of yourself who wants to quit and change the conversation.
4. **Build Your Wall.** Build your wall one brick at a time. Once it's complete, you may be unrecognizable.

16.
ESSENTIAL
HABITS

"Leave all the afternoon for exercise and recreation, which are as necessary as reading. I will rather say more necessary because health is worth more than learning."
Thomas Jefferson

Achieving extraordinary results through killing comfort requires three habits. First, you must adopt the daily habit of hormesis. Hormesis is applying just enough stress in your life so that you are propelled to higher levels. Second, you must continually seek out hard things. Nothing is worse than never being challenged. We all face challenges in life, but the hard things we propose are challenges you impose on yourself. And last, you must find your one thing, to make big and small decisions easier. Pursue these three habits daily over decades and you are on the path to extraordinary results.

16. ESSENTIAL HABITS

THE THREE HABITS OF KILLING COMFORT

1. The Hormesis Habit
2. Pursue Hard Things
3. Live by Your One Thing

HORMESIS

Friedrich Nietzsche's simple statement, "That which does not kill us makes us stronger," speaks of a truth in many different areas of our lives. In 1943, this concept entered the scientific lexicon known today, as hormesis.

In the fields of biology and medicine, hormesis is defined as an adaptive response of cells and organisms to a moderate (usually intermittent) stress. Examples most practiced today include:

- Extreme Heat Exposure (sauna use)
- Physical Exercise
- Cold Exposure
- Dietary Energy Restriction (fasting)

Hormesis triggers a vast array of protective mechanisms that not only repair cell damage, but also provide protection from subsequent exposures to more devastating stressors.

To put hormesis in simple terms, a little is good for you, and too much will kill you...thanks, Nietzsche!

And some form of hormesis is something I think you should do every day. When you properly balance your life with the EO3 Elements introduced earlier in this book, you are more apt to take on a hormesis habit.

Hormesis comes in many forms, but we still haven't found a more potent and beneficial form of hormesis than that of simple, but boring, physical fitness. In fact, most of the benefits seen with cold or heat exposure and even fasting are also seen with exercise.

Being that fitness is my life's work, I could write books on the intricacies of different types of fitness for different goals. However, in this book, my goal is to give you a simple, practical philosophy that you can use for the rest of your life.

I want you to build a strong foundation through controlled strength work and aerobic conditioning. Nothing fancy. Controlled strength training and aerobic (oxidative) conditioning. That's it. If you only want to be healthy, i.e., live longer, be a little bit stronger, be able to move better, etc., you could do only these two simple things in perpetuity.

When you perform different training at different intensities, your body uses different fuel sources. Here's my crash course in bioenergetics. The lower the intensity, the more your body relies on fat, the higher the intensity, the more your body will depend on sugar. Additionally, every time you perform high-intensity training, you signal a cascade of hormones similar to when you do heavy lifting. Some of these hormones are good and necessary for continued progress. However, some hormones, released repeatedly every day, can have some pretty adverse effects. Consistently elevated cortisol levels combined with living a high-cortisol/high-stress life, will spell eventual disaster.

We've seen it with athletes over and over. It starts subtly. At first, you just don't feel as recovered. Then, you begin to notice you are getting sick more often. Finally, you may just not feel as motivated, in general, as you usually do. The problem is that a type-A personality sees this as an opportunity to double down on what is creating the problem in the first place by increasing intensity!

This "do more" and "go harder" mentality is not supported by scientific evidence. If you were to plot how often and how hard you train on a horizontal axis and how many upper respiratory infections (URI) on a vertical axis, you would produce a J-shaped curve. The graph shows if you don't train at all, or live a sedentary lifestyle, you can expect to get sick an average number of times, i.e., about as often as the general public. If you train regularly, but not excessively, you can expect to get sick about half as many times as the sedentary individual. The interesting part is at the top of the J-Curve. Those who train too hard, or too frequently, get sick twice as often as the sedentary individuals. More is not always better. Again, a little is good for you and too much will kill you.

If you are reading this book and you are not in the best shape or possibly even bordering on Metabolic Syndrome (MtS), then you probably want to burn fat.

If your metabolic health is poor, your body will have a harder time burning fat because your cells' mitochondria aren't used to using fat efficiently as a source of energy.

You will have a decreased ability to burn fat, you will transition very early from fat as a fuel source to carbohydrates as a fuel source, and you will experience an increase in lactate at lower intensities compared to someone who is better trained.

If you are in this situation, your sweet spot will be Zone 2 training. When your heart rate is 60% to 70% of your maximum heart rate, then you are in training in Zone 2. This is just simple aerobic training, as I have already suggested, but with a parameter to make sure you are doing things correctly. In Zone 2, you will improve the efficiency of your mitochondria and burn more fat.

Now, heart rate zones are basically estimates, so here are some other guidelines. First, when performing aerobic training in Zone 2, you should still be able to hold a conversation—this will be walking for a lot of people. Second, there should be little to no muscle burn. When your muscles burn, that means lactate is present, and lactate is correlated with poor fat oxidation (fat burn) and higher carbohydrate use—which we are trying to stay away from. Now, there is no need to run from muscle burn in your strength training, only in your aerobic Zone 2-based training when you are intentionally trying to burn fat.

So, to simplify all this, I am basically saying walk and lift weights.

If you are reading this book and you are in great shape, I still suggest Zone 2 training, since burning fat and mitochondrial health is good for you no matter your level of fitness. Iñigo San Millán, Ph.D., who has spent his career studying elite cyclists, states that 60% to 75% of a cyclist's entire training time is spent inside of Zone 2.

And if you do want to pursue more intense training, as our athletes do sparingly, then I have two suggestions. First, your recovery is of the utmost importance, and dialing in the elements mentioned earlier in this book should be at the forefront of your training regimen. Second, when performing high-intensity training, rest more between intense bouts. This will allow your body to practice its metabolic flexibility by using different fuel sources throughout your activity and help your body practice clearing lactate.

Simple strength training and low-intensity aerobic training are beneficial no matter your current level of fitness and are essential for every human looking to improve their quality of life and health span.

If you are more advanced and would like to dive deeper into our energy system training protocols and our utilization of different strength methods, please visit EndofThreeFitness.com for free articles and resources on this topic.

HARD THING

To begin the day on the right foot, Benjamin Franklin would ask himself this question: "What good shall I do this day?" It was one of his goals in life to attain "moral perfection." He admittedly never achieved the perfection he sought, but the goal and attempt were noble nonetheless.

For our purposes, I want you to ask yourself a different question each day.

"What hard thing shall I do this day?

Recall our hard things equation: Pushing Forward Against Your Own Desire + Daily Over Decades = Hard Thing.

One of the great Stoics, Marcus Aurelius, wrote:

> "Our actions may be impeded, but there can be no impeding our intentions or dispositions. Because we can accommodate and adapt. The mind adapts and converts to its own purposes the obstacle to our acting. The impediment to action advances action. What stands in the way becomes the way."

Pursuing hard things acts as a compass. You will encounter big decisions and insurmountable tasks in your life that will seem impossible, but these things you don't want to do will become the things you must do for continued progress.

But you won't be ready for them when they come if you don't practice. Starting today. The hard thing I want you to pursue each day doesn't have to be a massive task like running a marathon or writing a book.

Each day, I simply want you to do something you absolutely do not want to do. I want you to push forward against your own desire, daily.

This could be doing the dishes at the end of a very hard day, it could be a workout, it could be journaling, meditating. What constitutes a hard thing will be different for everyone.

When you do a hard thing, you push against your natural tendency. For instance, I love working out. It has been a habitual thing for me for over 15 years. So, for me to say my hard thing today was a difficult training session, I would be lying. I love training. It goes *with* my desire, not against it.

Now, doing the hard thing is only 50% of the battle. The real benefits are realized when you control your inner chatter while you are doing the hard thing. If you really don't want to do your selected hard thing...change your conversation.

Once you realize you are in control of your mental chatter, and you can guide the conversation in your head, you will start to change your life drastically.

Managing this internal dialogue while pursuing hard things is the ultimate challenge.

ONE THING

We've already covered Rockefeller's one thing as it pertained to his business, however it wasn't his only one thing. Rockefeller believed his path to business success and wealth was divinely ordained. Rockefeller's personal and spiritual beliefs formed the one thing that he is best known for today, his philanthropy. You can have a different one thing for each area of your life and you can even revise/update your one thing over time.

Discovering your one thing can take days, weeks, or even months to be entirely comfortable with the deliberation and decision—this process is not comfortable, and few will do it. However, once you have a guiding mission statement, decisions get a whole lot easier.

When others comfortably jump from one thing to another, you will stay focused on your North Star. Finding your one thing, and sticking to your one thing, is key. Chasing the next big thing will lead to failure and missed opportunities.

For some of you, determining your one thing will be easy, because you already know what it is. You have it written down somewhere, or you feel it in your bones and have never given it a name. What do you come back to over and over? Is there a theme? Is there a pattern?

If you are struggling to start the journey towards finding your one thing, simply determine where you want to go. Reverse engineer the big picture of your life and ask, "What are the steps to get there?"

From there, your more immediate next steps will become clear. Taking these next steps will reveal your one thing. Over time, a pattern will emerge. Your career choices, your skills, and your passion will coalesce into a distinct one thing.

For me, my ONE Thing always comes back to helping make better humans. This one thing takes lots of forms. This is MY one thing.

From what I write, to how I run my business, to how I parent my children—if it isn't consistent with building a better human, I don't do it.

Back to you. What's your one thing?

Pursue these three habits and you may just change your life. The people who see extraordinary results are a culmination of their daily habits. They achieve success through a few simple actions repeated on a long enough timeline. Those with sporadic efforts of intensity across multiple domains will make little progress...but they are fun to watch!

TAKEAWAYS

1. **Hormesis.** Pursue a proper dose of stress, not too much and not too little, to see continued progress in all areas of your life.
2. **Keep it Simple.** It is both extremely simple and complex. Pursue the basics, keep it simple by lifting weights and participating in aerobic conditioning. The best way to use hormesis for better health and fitness is to cover all the bases.
3. **Change the Conversation.** If you can control your thoughts, you can change your life.
4. **Follow the Clues.** Your life, your goals, your choices, your motivation—they leave clues. Piece together the clues, and you will find your purpose...your ONE THING.

17.
MISTAKES

"Improvement isn't inevitable. Change is." Unknown

Carl Von Clausewitz introduced us to the idea of the "fog of war " in his book, _On War_.

The fog of war is inherent in the nature of war. It can take many forms—friction, ambiguity, chaos, uncertainty, or combinations of any.

Many costly mistakes are made under the fog of war.

In the military, one way to combat the fog of war is to delegate decision making to the lowest level necessary. Or as Sun Tzu put it, "When you see the correct course, act; do not wait for orders."

The fog of war does not typically happen at the highest level. It happens in the execution, during battle, when the plan goes from paper to action.

17. MISTAKES

So far, I have given you a lot of big ideas to work on and ideas to implement. While the ideas are sound, you could get lost in the daily doing.

In life, we battle a similar fog. And to fight through it, you will need to recognize mistakes and avoid them. You'll know what to do and what to steer clear of as you take the words of this book and translate them into actions.

Just as there are six traps that can unknowingly ease you into comfort, there are four mistakes that can ruin your Killing Comfort Journey.

THE FOUR MISTAKES OF KILLING COMFORT

1. Misuse of Discipline "Physics"
2. Complaining
3. Indecisiveness
4. Failure to Understand the Dichotomy of Comfort

1. DISCIPLINE PHYSICS

A Russian commander said in a report, after pulling out of Chechnya in the first Russian-Chechen War, that he could trace the defeat back to one moment in time: when the men stopped shaving.

Despite having more men, air support, and power, it was this small break in discipline this commander recognized as the beginning of the end.

Not many would argue the importance of discipline in achieving success. Without discipline you will fail to kill comfort. Self-control, by definition, is a form of killing comfort. It's not always easy to push yourself to do something you don't desire.

I am not only urging you to be disciplined, but to be aware of any breakdown in discipline. It might be one seemingly insignificant action or inaction—something you don't view as important, so you stop doing it. This could be the beginning of your unraveling.

The very nature of discipline implies that you are forcing yourself to do something that you do not want to do. Now, you may want what discipline provides. You may even like some of the activities that require discipline. But, for the most part, you are forcing yourself to do something.

The harder you push into life the harder it will push back. It will not be forever. It will not always be life or death or the hardest thing you have ever done. But, if you press into life it WILL press back.

Discipline is physics.

Part 1: A motion at rest tends to stay at rest, unless an outside force acts upon it.

We are slaves to this rule.

It is so much easier to sit on the couch rather than do the dishes. It is easier to stay in bed rather than get up and hit a workout.

17. MISTAKES

If you're not careful, your whole life will end up this way. You'll look back at the end and wonder, "What have I accomplished?"

Unfortunately for most of us, the answer will be, "Not much."

You have to be the force that acts. You have to put yourself into motion, and because we live in a world governed by the laws of physics, you will then have to produce work. Work takes energy, it expends calories, and it acts contrary to the very thing our mind and bodies have been conditioned to do for generations: conserve and survive.

But you have to PUSH. And that leads us to Part 2 of discipline.

Part 2: For every action there is an opposite and equal reaction.

When you have decided to be more disciplined. Nature will react to your force.

Small goals, small steps, and small ideas are met with small resistance.

If you are just starting down this journey, start small. Celebrate small wins and defeat resistance one small step at a time.

An athlete doesn't squat 500 pounds without first successfully performing a bodyweight squat. No, increasing the weight by small increments allows the athlete to achieve the goal.

17. MISTAKES

But, there will come a time when you are able to overcome small resistance.

In the same way that a muscle can be trained to lift progressively heavier weights, once your body has adapted to performing a specific task or tasks, it is time to increase the weight, so to speak.

Keep in mind that big goals, big steps, and big ideas are met with BIG resistance.

This is why the "overhaul never works."

You know what I am talking about. You get all psyched up, maybe at the start of a new year, after a conference or reading a great book and you decide that tomorrow is the day!!

You set off with 37 new habits, a new workout routine, a new diet approach and you plan to wake up and go to bed earlier.

Just one problem.

You haven't built up enough "strength" to overcome this level of resistance.

You may be able to grit your teeth and get through a day, a week, or maybe even a month.

But, eventually, you will be crushed.

You didn't train properly. You don't deserve what you were trying to achieve. You haven't earned it.

Match your level of challenge to the level of discipline you possess. Too easy, it won't be the stimulus you need for growth. Too hard, and you will be crushed and never move forward.

2. COMPLAINING

On this journey of Killing Comfort, do not complain.

We are full of complaints: my arm hurts, I didn't get that promotion, I can't lose weight.

Typically, we complain about a desire. Something we want. If your arm hurts, you complain. You desire an arm without pain. But where does it end? When will you be complaint free?

To best illustrate this, there is an old fable involving a grandfather and his grandson who set out to work their land.

On that day, they were to build a fence. Some serious labor. Digging holes, hammering in posts, and carrying heavy objects. This would be enough for most people to complain about.

But, the grandson had a toothache. Every time he swung the hammer and struck the post, he would get a shooting pain in his tooth clear through to his jaw.

He complained to the grandfather all day saying, "If only my tooth was better, I would not complain anymore. I would enjoy this work."

Months passed and his tooth got better. It was winter, and the boy and his grandfather were working on a carpentry project. The boy spent the morning cursing the cold and telling his grandfather about his numb finger tips.

The grandfather then asked, "How's your tooth?" To which the boy responded, "Oh, it's fine." The grandfather said, "What a remarkable day this must be!"

The truth is that there can be no good without bad. There can be no light without darkness.

Now, I am not saying that if something good happens to you that you should also expect something bad to come with it.

But, I am telling you to appreciate the journey. Discomfort is part of the journey and not worthy of a complaint.

We don't sit around and talk about breathing, our heart beating or our hair growing—that is all part of living.

Every time you don't want to get out of bed. Every time you don't want to train. Every time your day presents you with more obstacles than expected, know that it's part of the process.

I am not suggesting that you pretend that your life is perfect every minute of the day. I am suggesting that you change your perception.

If you need to talk about a problem or grievance you can, but it needs to immediately be followed with a proposed solution.

Then, I can guarantee two things will happen:

1. The people around you will enjoy your lack of complaints and if you state a problem with an immediate solution, they'll like that too.
2. You'll realize that you can propose a solution, or act on one, without ever having to state the complaint in the first place; you can just fix your situation.

This takes time and practice, but you can start by taking steps in the right direction.

3. INDECISIVENESS

You have to decide.

No one will give it to you, you have to go get it for yourself!

You have to decide that what you are after is, in fact, what you want. It sounds simple but I see indecision everywhere I go. How well do you make decisions? How quickly? If I asked you what you want out of life, what would your response be?

If you lack a response, you haven't decided. Decision takes courage and faith.

And, it doesn't stop there.

Commitment and perseverance are on the other side of a decision and will be an even tougher battle than making the decision itself.

You have little time to waste on indecisiveness. Decide now.

4. FAILURE TO UNDERSTAND THE DICHOTOMY

Not every uncomfortable action is worth pursuing.

If you were to sleep for just three hours, one night, on the floor you would give yourself an opportunity—the kind of opportunity that would make you appreciate your normal life, allow you to get some perspective, and foster some mental fortitude through discomfort.

However, sleep 3 to 4 hours per night for years on end, and the story has a different ending. Yes, it would be very uncomfortable but also a great way to shorten your life. This is not discomfort worth pursuing.

There's the intentional pursuit of discomfort and then there's stupidity. But, to make matters worse, chasing discomfort is a tricky task. A tricky task that involves a dichotomy.

I have a friend who started a very successful business. He did so by working through a lot of discomfort. He hustled and worked and by willpower and sheer force, he grew his business.

17. MISTAKES

This made him a productivity junkie. He trained himself to work hard and to work constantly. In fact, once he finally hired a rockstar team, he didn't take a break or ease off—he maintained all the same habits. He filled every moment of his time with tasks, no matter what. He never looked up, paused, or reflected.

Hard work enabled him to achieve beyond the norm. His business had experienced robust growth...until now. He called me, confused. Despite all of his hard work, his business had stopped growing.

This is where killing comfort gets very tricky and where the dichotomy exists. My friend had become very accustomed to discomfort. His discomfort allowed him to maintain a high-level of productivity aimed towards a specific goal. Because his business grew and achieved success, these behaviors were reinforced by the growth and success of his business. But, like I said, he had hired a team. A team who was capable of running every aspect of the business without him.

Since I'm also an entrepreneur, he asked me to take a look at his business from an outsider's perspective. For me, the reason why his business stopped growing was obvious. It's always simple when someone asks me what they should do next, no matter the goal. I look for the area of discomfort, like a compass pointing towards true north, then I suggest doubling down in that area.

After looking at his daily business operations, overall efficiency, and daily workload I could see there was nothing more he could do. There was no slack to take up. Sooooo, my advice shocked him. I told him that he needed to do less.

At first, he didn't like this advice at all. He didn't think it would be possible to grow his business by doing less. He had been operating at such a high level of productivity for so long—these habits ingrained in him—that operating at this level was actually comfortable.

Doing less would put him in an unfamiliar area. An area of pure discomfort. I told him the goal of doing less was not to sit on his hands and do nothing. He was focusing on daily tasks that packed very little punch, yet made him feel super productive. I told him to get off the hamster wheel of productivity. I asked him to take a step back, see the big picture and reflect on the steps he would need to take to resuscitate his business. What he needed to do was a lot of thinking and planning, less doing.

At first, this made him very uncomfortable, but he did it anyway. He chased a new area of discomfort. Within a few weeks, he had relinquished all of his busy work. This gave him time to develop a plan to franchise his business and to grow it beyond what he could manage himself. He even took on a new role coaching those in the same field to new levels of success, becoming part of a business that will soon dwarf his original model.

He pursued discomfort, did less, and achieved more. Discomfort comes cloaked in many forms and chasing it isn't always as easy as it sounds. My friend is not the norm, and so I assume most readers of this book need to start by becoming comfortable with the doing part. This said, you always need to be aware of your comfort level and constantly ask yourself, "Am I taking the right steps towards discomfort right now?"

You'll be surprised at how often this dichotomy reveals itself as you live a life of killing comfort, so pay attention and don't miss it. When results start to stall, you may not be pursuing the correct form of discomfort any longer.

TAKEAWAYS

1. **Discipline.** Push against a level of resistance you can withstand. Be honest with yourself about what that may be.
2. **Complaints.** Discomfort is part of the journey, so don't waste your breath complaining about it.
3. **Decide.** Every accomplishment starts with a decision to act. You need to decide quickly for there is much work to be done after the decision is made.
4. **Dichotomy.** Don't pursue stupid uncomfortable tasks and blame this book. By doing so, you will prove you have missed the message contained therein! Look for the next area of growth, where things may be slowing down, to understand which discomfort to chase.

18.

COMFORT IS THE ENEMY, A CALL TO ARMS

"Comfortable choices are killing you."
The Person You Could Be

Comfort is the enemy.

If we don't kill comfort, comfort will kill us. Comfort zaps dreams, ideas, and potential out of many. So, when we talk about killing comfort, I'm not merely talking about getting off the couch. I'm talking about realizing your full potential, and the only way to do that is to continually put yourself in uncomfortable positions.

I live in a world where people argue about the best diets and training programs, but they are all missing

189

the point. If one is too comfortable to precipitate change, the method of change is inconsequential.

There are many ways to kill comfort: moving your body (fitness), taking a second to breathe, deciding on healthy food options, controlling your thoughts, starting a business, being a good parent, etc.

Killing comfort is simple. Never lie on your back, submissive to what life throws your way. Always resist, push back. So long as you have air in your lungs, you give an effort worthy of who you are. The very act of pushing back is killing comfort because applying force against resistance is uncomfortable.

This idea is at the fulcrum of the lever. Whether you lean toward comfort or discomfort, you will do so by a razor-thin margin. Most people choose comfort and become mindless robots who use pacifiers. Adult pacifiers that get you to shut up and stay average are things like cell phones, the TV, and whatever else keeps you in the status quo of mediocrity. The pursuit of discomfort is a continuous life-long battle.

You already have the fire in you to succeed on this path. There are a lot of people in this world telling you how things should be done. It's this program, that diet. It's a shot of 6-pack abs on a beach. It's a celebrity endorsement. It's your favorite athlete telling you through social media what diet they follow. It's another picture of a half-naked social media influencer. There are a lot of people in this world telling you how things should be done.

But what does it take??

The secret is action. It's not what you do today. It's what you do every SINGLE day. But we can't start there.

Not yet.

First, you have to KNOW. You have to know it is 100% possible to achieve your goals. Yes, what and how you do things matters. But if you don't think you can make it, everything else is useless.

You can do this.

It doesn't matter what you say or why you think you can't. Say it to me, and my response will always be the same. You can do this.

"Jerred, you don't know how many times I have tried..."

You can do this.

"Jerred, I can't stay motivated. It works for a little while, but then everything falls apart..."

You can do this.

"Jerred, you don't know my schedule, my life, or what I face daily..."

You can do this.

You can change little by little, just one thing at a time. It will feel forced and awkward, and you may even hate it. But, it will start to work. Making a change won't be fun. You may not enjoy pushing yourself or trying to find the time to fit new things into your schedule, but the results will start to show.

What you cannot do is sit around and twiddle your thumbs.

You have to DO something!

Don't feel sorry for yourself or think about how you will never achieve your goals. You have to do something!

Believe in yourself. Believe in your ability to achieve your goal. It's that simple.

Killing comfort will be more challenging for some than others, but that doesn't mean you shouldn't pursue your goals. If you know you can do this and you're ready to do it, then good—this book was the easy part of the journey. Worse case scenario, this book was a complete waste of your time because you aren't prepared to take massive action. If you are ready to take action, welcome to Killing Comfort.

ON THE RESEARCH

I've been obsessed with the idea of how to get people to start and then stick to things, for over a decade. My quest, which ultimately ended up in the pages of this book, started in 2012. Since then, I have accumulated thousands of scientific studies, scholarly articles, and academic papers. I've conducted hundreds of expert interviews and accumulated a large library of books. And, after working with thousands of people, I've filled notebooks full of data and anecdotal findings. During the writing of this book, the research for it covered every square inch of my office.

However, my research is not complete, and it never will be, because understanding human behavior is an elusive pursuit. If you want to dive deeper into topics covered in this book, you can find a list of references and my continued research efforts at KillingComfort.com.

You'll also find resources, downloads, and tools created to support you on your path to Killing Comfort. Enjoy the journey.

ABOUT THE AUTHOR

Jerred Moon is a coach and author. He dedicates himself to the study of leadership and has served as Captain in the U.S. Air Force, leading teams throughout his career. After leaving active duty, Jerred became a certified strength and conditioning coach and founded his company, End of Three Fitness, with the aim to build better humans and redefine how fitness programs are written. The award-winning and best-selling author of "The Garage Gym Athlete," Jerred is recognized as one of the most influential leaders in the fitness industry. He is the founder of Better Human Business, a consulting company that helps scale businesses dedicated to improving the lives of others. He and his family live in a small town outside of Dallas, Texas.

ACKNOWLEDGMENTS

I am not unaware that I am standing on the shoulders of giants—titans of industry, scientific researchers, and the wise authors who came before me. I am indebted to them and to my mentors.

This book would not have been possible without the help of some amazing people. First, I want to thank my wife who supports me in everything I do and who provides me with the ability to pursue my passion. Also, my team at End of Three Fitness, who helped make this project a reality by keeping operations moving, so that I could focus solely on being an author. To my parents, who instilled a strong work ethic in me and always inspired me to be the best. I also owe a debt of gratitude to the thousands of athletes who trust me and my team to provide guidance and support on their fitness journeys. The insight I draw from each person in our community is immeasurable. It is our fitness community that drives me forward and inspires me every day. This book would not be what it is without the editing and valuable advice of my editor, Jonna Licata.

Finally, would it be weird to thank wolves? It was the discovery of how often a wolf fails, yet presses forward, that sparked the writing of this book. This fact coalesced with all my previous research to form one single idea: killing comfort.

LET'S CONNECT!

If you would like to continue the conversation about killing comfort, or learn about any of Jerred's other books, you can contact Jerred at:

Email: j@endofthreefitness.com
Online: JerredMoon.com

Facebook, Instagram, and Twitter profiles can be found at JerredMoon.com

To bring Killing Comfort or Jerred Moon to your organization—as United States Army Special Operations Command and United States Air Force Special Operations Command have—please go to JerredMoon.com/speaking.

To purchase bulk Copies of Killing Comfort and Jerred's other books at a discount for large groups or organizations, please contact support@endofthreefitness.com or call +1 214 513 3909.

Thanks for reaching out!